101 DELAWARE WING-T PLAYS

Harold R. "Tubby" Raymond
Ted Kempski

COACHES CHOICE

ISBN: 1-57167-163-3
Library of Congress Catalog Card Number: 97-80943

Cover Design: Deborah M. Bellaire
Front Cover Photo: Elsburgh Clarke Photography
Diagrams: James Hunt
Developmental Editor: Joanna Wright; Jeff Walker
Production Manager: Michelle A. Summers

Coaches Choice Books is a division of: Sagamore Publishing, Inc.
                                           P.O. Box 647
                                           Champaign, IL 61824-0647
                                           Web Site: http//www.sagamorepub.com

DEDICATION

This book is dedicated to all the fine young men who
established the football tradition and played for us at the
University of Delaware.

ACKNOWLEDGMENTS

We are deeply indebted to the coaches who taught football with us during my tenure as head football coach at the University of Delaware.

Marty Apostolico	Ted Kempski
Herky Billings	Otto Kneidinger
Paul Billy	David Lockwood
Bryan Bossard	Jeff Lukas
Tom Coder	Ed Maley
David Cohen	Josh Mastrangelo
Tony DeMeo	Jim McCarthy
Bob Depew	Mike Miller
Kevin Dickerson	Gregg Perry
Mike DiMartile	Joe Purzycki
R.B. "Scotty" Duncan	Chris Raymond
Jimmy Flynn	Ron Rogerson
Tony Glenn	Warren Ruggerio
Ted Gregory	Bob Sabol
Jim Grube	Greg Ventresca
Marshall Hall	Steve Verbit
Eric Hammack	Matt Wildes
Don Harnum	Irvin Wisniewski
Mickey Heinecken	Bob Wolford

CONTENTS

Chapter

PREFACE

We wrote this series of five books, *The Delaware Wing-T: The Running Game, The Option Game and the Passing Game, 101 Delaware Wing-T Drills,* and *101 Delaware Wing-T Plays* to provide coaches at all competitive levels with tools to enable them to better understand and implement the Delaware Wing-T. Each volume is designed to complement the other four books.

Volume 1 examines how to institute an effective running game with the Delaware Wing-T offense. Volumes 2 and 3 present an overview of how we employ an option attack and a passing attack, respectively, from the Delaware Wing-T. Volume 4 provides 101 drills for developing, practicing and refining the various essential fundamentals and techniques that are integral to the Delaware Wing-T. Finally, Volume 5 includes 101 basic plays that can be incorporated into a Delaware Wing-T offensive system.

Collectively, we hope that these books will provide you with the insights, the information and the foundation needed to fully comprehend and utilize the Delaware Wing-T. Properly executed, this unique offense can enable you to take advantage of your players' specific talents and skills in a goal-oriented, creative way.

Football is a great game. As a metaphor for life, football involves many of the critical elements that are required for success in almost any undertaking—sacrifice, hard work, teamwork, planning and an unrelenting commitment to excellence. To the extent that this series of five books (and a companion series of five instructional videos) enables you—in some small way—to appreciate this terrific game even more, then our efforts to write these volumes and to produce these videos will have been well worthwhile.

Harold R. "Tubby" Raymond
Ted Kempski

CHAPTER 1

PERIMETER PLAYS

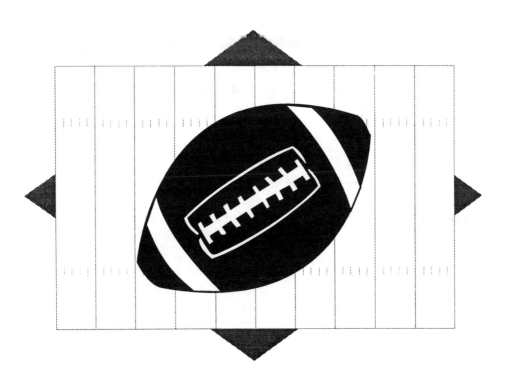

Play #1—"Tight 121"

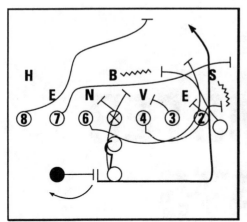

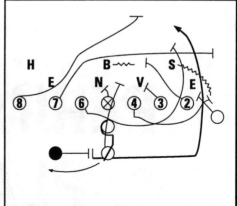

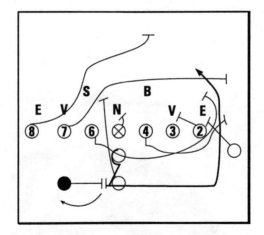

Blocking Rules:

2— Spread: Stalk 1
    Unbalance: Stalk 1
    Slot: Down
    Tight: Gap—down—backer
3— Gap—down—backer
    (Check wide tackle 6 backer)
4— Pull block out on first man
    outside of RH's block
5— Reach—left
6— Pull—wall off
7— Cut off
8— Spread: Cut off
    Tight: Cut off

Backfield Coaching Points:

QB— Reverse pivot—follow mid-line—hand
      off to LH—bootleg left
LH— Carrier: Receive hand off
RH— Block first free man inside
FB— Dive for left foot of 5 man—fake 24 Gut

Play #2—"929"

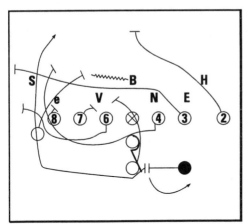

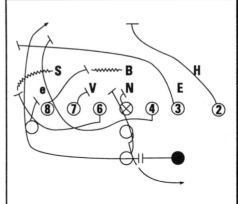

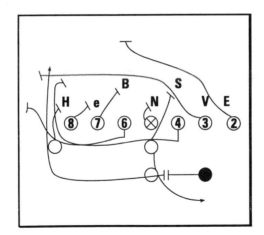

Blocking Rules:

2— Spread: Cut off
   Tight: Cut off
3— Cut off
4— Pull—wall off
5— Reach—right
6— Pull—block out on first man outside of
   LH's block (split—first man outside of
   end's block)
7— Gap—down—backer
8— Spread: Stalk 1
   Unbalance: Stalk 1
   Slot: Down
   Tight: Gap—down—backer

Backfield Coaching Points:

QB—Reverse pivot—follow mid-line—hand
    off to RH—bootleg right
LH— Block first free man inside
RH— Carrier: Receive hand off
FB— Dive for right foot of 5 man—fake 26
    Gut

Play #3— "921"

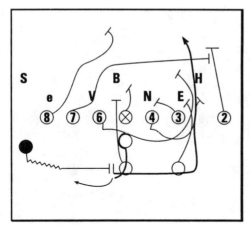

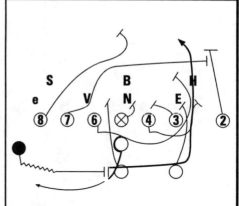

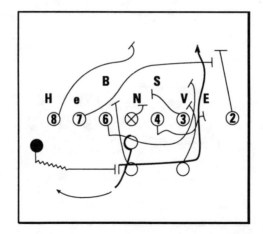

Blocking Rules:

2— Spread: Stalk 1
   Unbalance: Stalk 1
   Slot: Down
   Tight: Gap—down—backer
3— Gap—down—backer
   (Check wide tackle 6 backer)
4— Pull—block out on first man
   outside of RH's block
5— Reach—left
6— Pull—wall off
7— Cut off
8— Spread: Cut off
   Tight: Cut off

Backfield Coaching Points:

QB— Reverse pivot—follow mid-line—hand
     off to LH—bootleg left
LH— Carrier: Receive hand off
RH— Block first free man inside
FB— Dive for left foot of 5 man—fake 24 Gut

Play #4—"129"

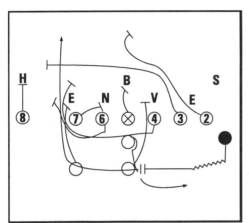
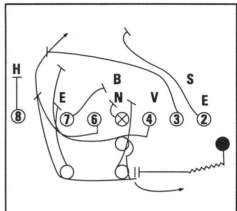
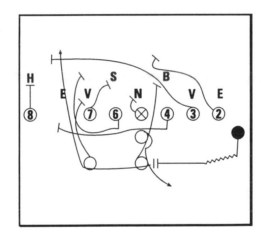

Blocking Rules:

2— Spread: Cut off
Tight: Cut off
3— Cut off
4— Pull—wall off
5— Reach—right
6— Pull—block out on first man outside of LH's block (split—first man outside of end's block)
7— Gap—down—backer
8— Spread: Stalk 1
Unbalance: Stalk 1
Slot: Down
Tight: Gap—down—backer

Backfield Coaching Points:

QB— Reverse pivot—follow mid-line—hand off to RH—bootleg right
LH— Block first free man inside
RH— Carrier: Receive hand off
FB— Dive for right foot of 5 man—fake 26 Gut

Play #5—"131"
Variations: "Spread 131"; "131 Gap"

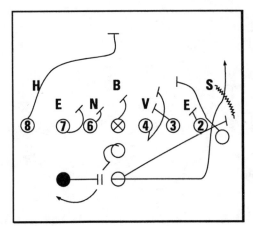
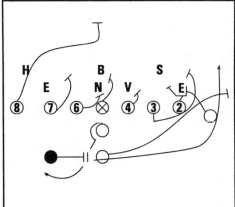

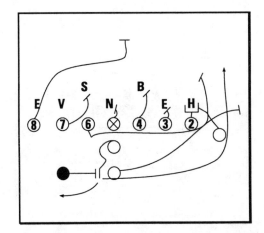

Blocking Rules:

2— Spread: Crack 2—stalk 1
Split: Down
Gap—conditional—post—read

3— Reach—on—backer (4 man may gut 3 man single gap with "bump" call)—pull if uncovered

4— Reach—on—backer (4 man may gut 3 man single gap with "bump" call)

5— Reach—on—backer (area left with 6 call)

6— Reach—on—backer (pull with 6 call)

7— Pull—check

8— Cut off (short yardage or goal line—pull check)

Backfield Coaching Points:

QB—Reverse pivot—follow mid-line—hand off to LH—bootleg left

LH— Carrier

RH— Block first free man inside

FB— Head for tail of 2 man—block first man outside of RH's—block either way

Play #6—"939"
Variations: "Spread 939"; "939 Gap"

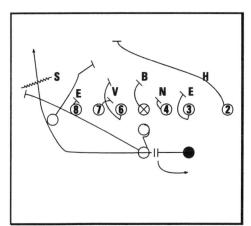

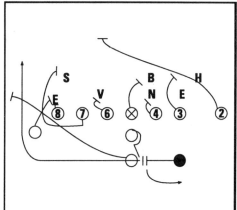

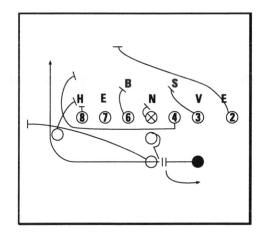

Blocking Rules:

2— Cut off (short yardage or goal line—pull check)

3— Pull—check

4— Reach—on—backer (pull with 4 call)

5— Reach—on—backer (area right with 4 call)

6— Reach—on—backer (6 man may gut 7 man single gap with "bump" call)

7— Reach—on—backer (6 man may gut 7 man single gap with "bump" call) pull if uncovered

Backfield Coaching Points:

8— Spread: Crack 2—stalk 1
   Split: Down
   Tight: Gap—post—conditional—lead

QB—Reverse pivot—follow mid-line—hand off to RH—bootleg right

LH— Block first free man inside

RH— Carrier

FB— Head for tail of 8 man—block first man outside of LH's block either way

Play #7—"981 Option"

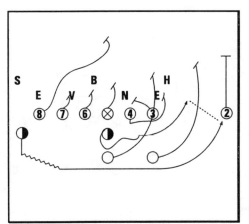

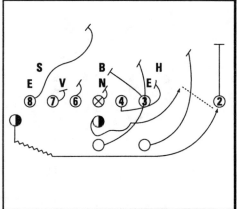

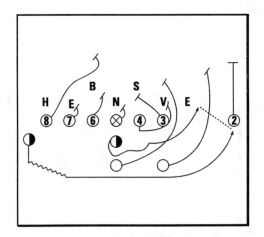

Blocking Rules:

2— Spread: Crack 2—stalk 1
  Tight with wing: Flare—block 1
3— Gap—down—backer (reach)
4— Pull—log first man on or outside of 3
  man (reach)
5— Reach—on—backer
6— Reach—on—backer
7— Reach—on—backer
8— Cut off

Backfield Coaching Points:

QB— Reverse pivot—ride ball sharply to FB—
  execute option
LH— Leave in early motion—be in position to
  receive pitch
RH— Wing: Flare outside of end man—stalk 1
  Slot or deep back: Flare—block 4
FB— Drive for outside foot of 3 man—turn up
  and block pursuit

Play #8—"189 Option"

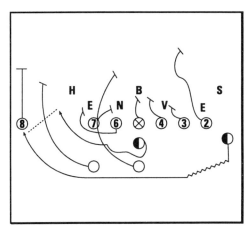

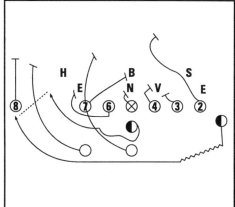

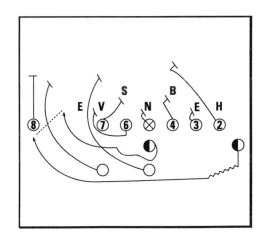

Blocking Rules:

2— Cut off
3— Reach—on—backer
4— Reach—on—backer
5— Reach—on—backer
6— Pull—log first man on or outside of 7 man (reach)
7— Gap—down—backer (reach)
8— Spread: Crack 2—stalk 1
   Tight with wing: Flare—block 1
   Tight without wing, split or slot:
   Release—stalk 1

Backfield Coaching Points:

QB— Reverse pivot—ride ball sharply to FB—execute option
LH— Wing: Flare outside of end man—stalk 2, Slot or deep back: Flare—block 2
RH— Leave in early motion—be in position to receive pitch
FB— Drive for outside foot of 7 man—turn up and block pursuit

Play #9—"981 Option Load"

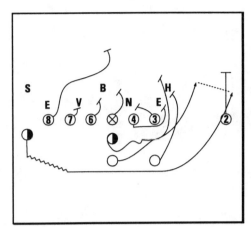
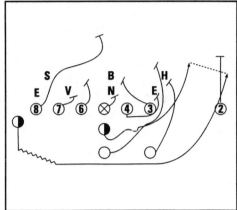
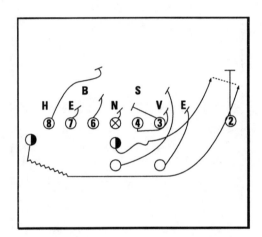

Blocking Rules:

2— Release—block outside defender
3— Gap—down—backer (reach)
4— Pull—log first man on or outside of 3 man (reach)
5— Reach—on—backer
6— Reach—on—backer
7— Reach—on—backer
8— Cut off

Backfield Coaching Points:

QB— Reverse pivot—ride ball sharply to FB— execute option
LH— Leave in early motion—be in position to receive pitch
RH— Dive outside tackle—block first man in area to inside
FB— Drive for outside foot of 3 man—turn up and block pursuit

Play #10—"189 Option Load"

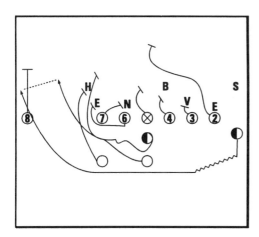 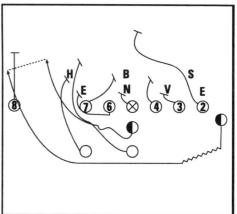

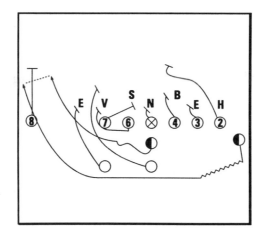

Blocking Rules:

2— Release—block outside defender
3— Reach—on—backer
4— Reach—on—backer
5— Reach—on—backer
6— Pull—log first man on or outside of 7 man (reach)
7— Gap—down—backer (reach)
8— Spread: Crack 2—stalk 1
   Tight with wing: Flare—block 1
   Tight without wing, split or slot:
   Release—stalk 1

Backfield Coaching Points:

QB— Reverse pivot—ride ball sharply to FB—execute option
LH— Dive outside tackle—block first man in area to inside
RH— Leave in early motion—be in position to receive pitch
FB— Drive for outside foot of 7 man—turn up and block pursuit

Play #11—"Spread 121 Trap Option"
Variations: "121 Trap Option Release"; "Z 121 Trap Option"

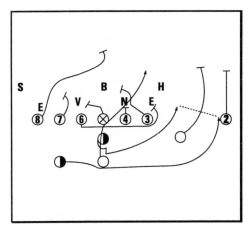

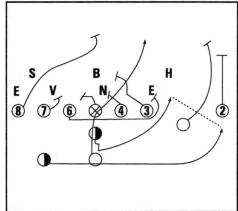

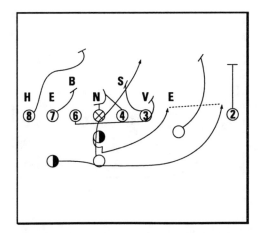

Blocking Rules:

2— Spread: Crack 2—stalk 1
3— Gap—bump—lead—backer
4— Gap—on—lead—backer
5— Post—left
6— Pull—log first man from outside foot of 3 man
7— Pull—check
8— Cut off

Backfield Coaching Points:

QB— Reverse pivot over mid-line for 2 steps— pause—then execute option
LH— Take off on snap—run option path—look for pitch
RH— Check 2—stalk 1
FB— Fake 23

Play #12—"Spread 929 Trap Option"
Variations: "929 Trap Option Release"; "Z 929 Trap Option"

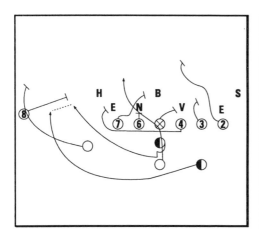

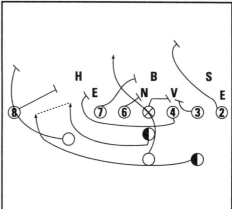

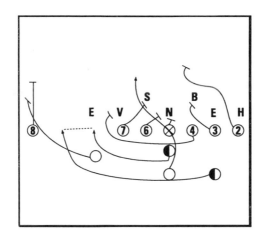

Blocking Rules:

2— Cut off
3— Pull—check
4— Pull—log first man from outside foot of 7 man
5— Post—right
6— Gap—on—lead—backer
7— Gap—bump—lead—backer
8— Spread: Crack 2—stalk 1
   Tight: Gap—backer

Backfield Coaching Points:

QB— Reverse pivot (over) mid-line for 2 steps—execute option
LH— Check 2—stalk 1
RH— Take off on snap—run option path—look for pitch
FB— Fake 27

Play #13—"Spread 141 Option"
Variation: "Spread 141 Option Gut"

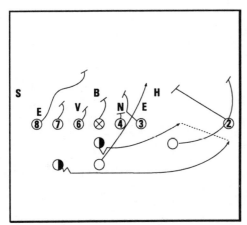
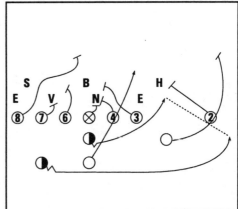

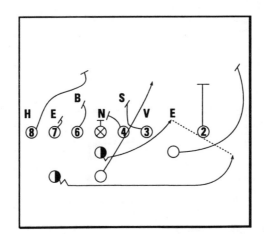

Blocking Rules:

2— Spread: Crack 2—stalk 1
  Tight with wing: Flare—block 1
  Tight without wing, split or slot:
  Release stalk 1

3— Gap—bump—lead—backer (block LB
  with gap call)

4— Gap—on—lead

5— Reach—on—backer (post vs. 55)

6— Reach—on—backer

7— Reach—on—backer

8— Cut off

Backfield Coaching Points:

QB— Step back—ride ball to FB—execute
  triple option

LH— Leave in one step motion—be in position
  to receive pitch

RH— Check 2—stalk 1. If three men are
  outside of 3 man—wall with two

FB— Dive for outside hip of 4 man—accept
  hand off or fake and block area

Play #14—"Spread 949 Option"
Variations: "Spread 949 Option Gut"; "Spread 949 Option Odd Gut"

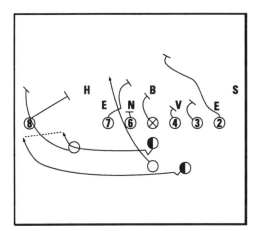

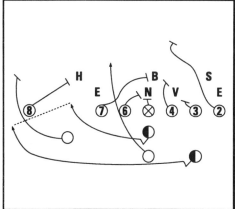

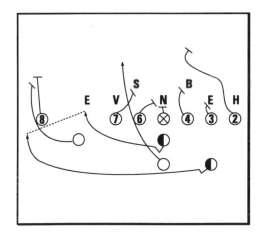

Blocking Rules:

2— Cut off
3— Reach—on—backer
4— Reach—on—backer
5— Reach—on—backer (post vs 55)
6— Gap—on—lead
7— Gap—bump—lead—backer (block LB with gap call)
8— Spread: Crack 2—stalk 1
   Tight with wing: Flare block 1
   Tight without wing, split or slot:
   Release—stalk 1

Backfield Coaching Points:

QB— Step back—ride ball to FB—execute triple option
LH— Check 2—stalk 1. If three men are outside 7 man—wall with two
RH— Leave in one step motion—be in position to receive pitch.
FB— Dive for outside hip of 6 man. Accept handoff or fake and block area.

Play #15—"Spread 131 Option Wall"

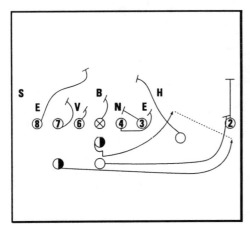
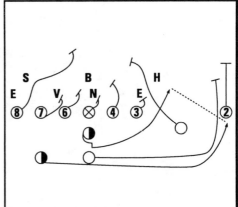

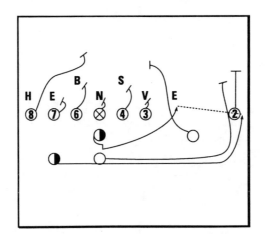

Blocking Rules:

2— Tight: Wall off
 Slot or split: Release—stalk 1
 Spread: Crack 2—stalk 1
3— Reach—on—backer
 (4 man may gut 3 man single gap)
4— Reach—on—backer
 (4 man may gut 3 man single gap)
5— Reach—on—backer
 (area left with 6 call)
6— Reach—on—backer
 (pull with 6 call)
7— Pull—check
8— Cut off (short yardage or goal line—pull
 check)

Backfield Coaching Points:

QB— Reverse pivot to mid-line for 2 steps—
 execute option
LH— Take off on snap—run option path—look
 for pitch
RH— Prevent penetration—wall off
FB— Flare—block support

Play #16—"Spread 939 Option Wall"

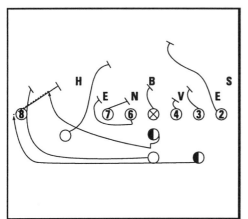
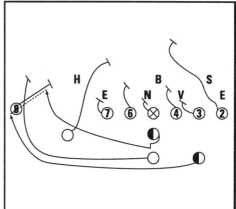

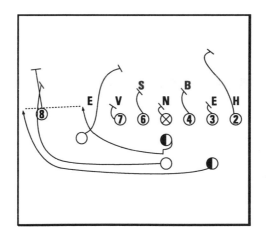

Blocking Rules:

2— Cut off (short yardage or goal line—pull check)

3— Pull—check

4— Reach—on—backer (pull with 4 call)

5— Reach—on—backer (area right with 4 call)

6— Reach—on—backer (6 man may gut 7 man single gap)

7— Reach—on—backer (6 man may gut 7 man single gap)

8— Tight: Wall off
Slot or split: Release—stalk 1
Spread: Crack 2—stalk 1

Backfield Coaching Points:

QB— Reverse pivot to mid-line for 2 steps— execute option

LH— Prevent penetration—wall off

RH— Take off on snap—run option path—look for pitch

FB— Flare—block support

Play #17—"Tight Spread 991 Option"
Variations: "Run to—Spread 991 Option (Load)"; "991 Option Pass"

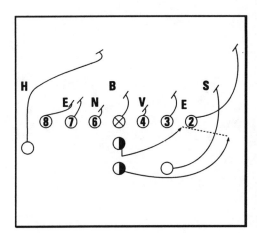

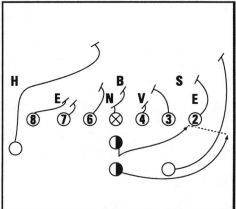

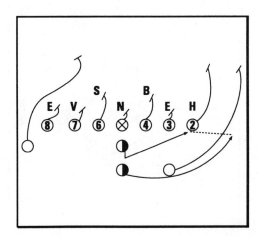

Blocking Rules:
2— Spread: Crack 2—stalk 1
   Tight: Release—stalk 2
3— Reach—on—backer
4— Reach—on—backer
5— Reach—on—backer
6— Reach—on—backer
7— Reach—on—backer
8— Cut off

Backfield Coaching Points:
QB— Take one step back—sprint right—
   execute option
LH— Cut off
RH— Flare—block 1
FB— Carrier: Sprint right—receive pitch

Play #18—"Spread 199 Option"
Variations: "Run to—Spread 199 Option (Load)"; "199 Option Pass"

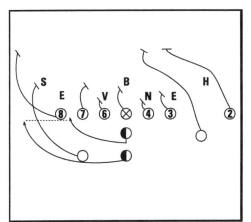
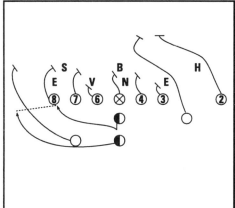
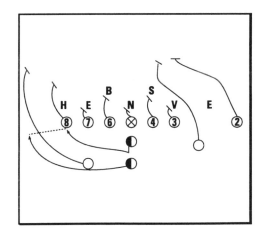

Blocking Rules:
2— Cut off
3— Reach—on—backer
4— Reach—on—backer
5— Reach—on—backer
6— Reach—on—backer
7— Reach—on—backer
8— Spread: Crack 2—stalk 1
   Tight: Release—stalk 2

Backfield Coaching Points:
QB— Take one step back—sprint left—
   execute option
LH— Flare—block 1
RH— Cut off
FB— Carrier: Sprint left—receive pitch

Play #19—"182 Option"
Variations: "142 Down Option"; "182 Down Option Load"

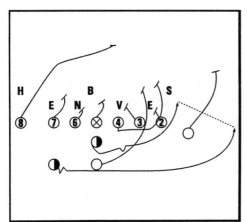

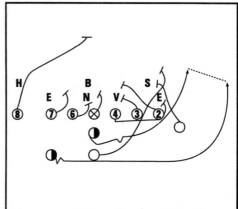

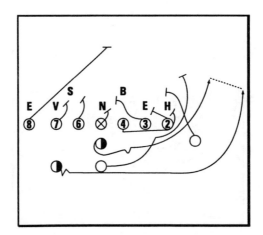

Blocking Rules:

2— Gap—down—backer
3— Gap—down—backer
4— Pull—log first man on or outside TE
5— Reach—on—backer
6— Reach—on—backer
7— Reach—on—backer
8— Cut off

Backfield Coaching Points:

QB— Reverse pivot—ride ball sharply to FB—execute option
LH— Leave in one step motion—be in position to receive pitch
RH— With one count—block first LB to inside. With two count—stalk 1
FB— Drive for inside foot of 2 man—block LB to FS

Play #20—"988 Down Option"
Variation: "948 Down Option"

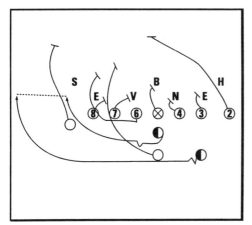

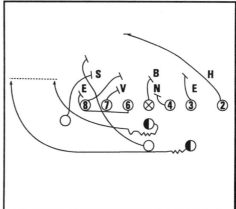

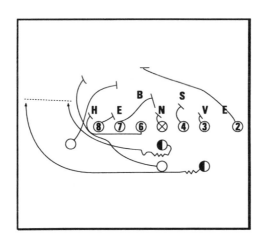

Blocking Rules:

2— Cut off
3— Reach—on—backer
4— Reach—on—backer
5— Reach—on—backer
6— Pull—log first man on or outside TE
7— Gap—down—backer
8— Gap—down—backer

Backfield Coaching Points:

QB—Reverse pivot—ride ball sharply to FB—
    execute option
LH— With one count—block first LB to
    inside. With two count—stalk 1
RH— Leave in one step motion—be in position
    to receive pitch
FB— Drive for inside foot of 8 man—block LB
    to FS

Play #21— "142 Option Gut"

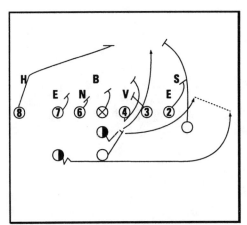
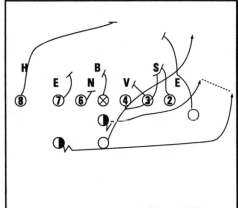

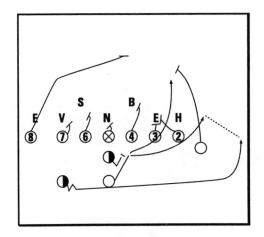

Blocking Rules:

2— Down—backer (outside release vs. bump—lead with 2 call)
3— Gap—down—backer (2 call with man on)
4— Pull—gut—backer to free safety (block LB with 2 call)
5— Reach—on—backer
6— Reach—on—backer
7— Reach—on—backer
8— Cut off

Backfield Coaching Points:

QB— Step back—ride ball to FB—execute veer option
LH— Leave in early motion—be in position to receive pitch
RH— Block LB to FS
FB— Dive for outside hip of 4 man—accept hand off or fake and block area

Play #22—"948 Option Gut"

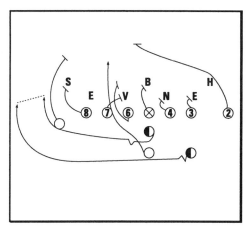

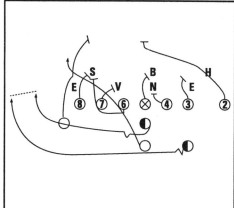

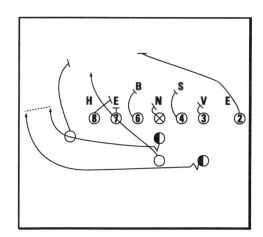

Blocking Rules:

2— Cut off
3— Reach—on—backer
4— Reach—on—backer
5— Reach—on—backer
6— Pull—gut—backer to free safety (block LB with 8 call)
7— Gap—down—backer (8 call with man on)
8— Down—backer (outside release vs. bump—lead with 8 call)

Backfield Coaching Points:

QB— Step back—ride ball to FB—execute veer option
LH— Block LB to FS
RH— Leave in early motion—be in position to receive pitch
FB— Dive for outside hip of 6 man—accept hand off or fake and block area

CHAPTER 2

OFF-TACKLE PLAYS

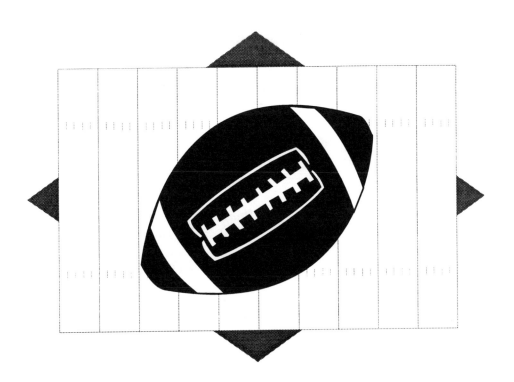

Play #23—"132"

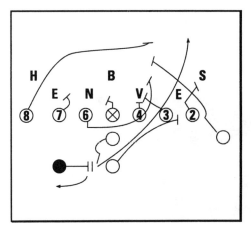
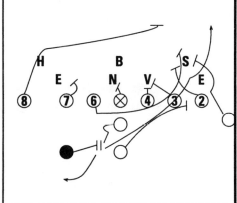

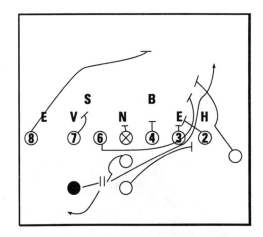

Blocking Rules:

2— Lead—backer—influence block right
3— Gap—post—lead
    (3 man will call "on", "short")
4— Gap—area—post
5— On—area—left
6— Pull—wall off
7— Pull—check
8— Out cut

Backfield Coaching Points:

QB— Reverse pivot—hand off—bootleg left
LH— Carrier: Run directly for hole
RH— Influence first man on or outside of 2
    man—wall off
FB— Head for tail of 3 man—block first man
    outside of 3 man

Play #24—"938"

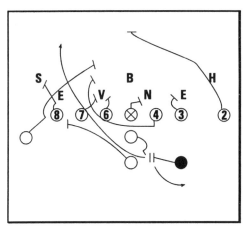

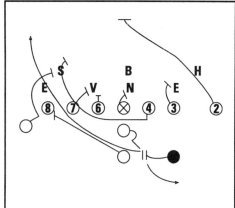

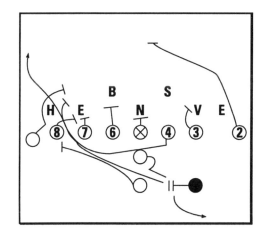

Blocking Rules:

2— Out cut
3— Pull—check
4— Pull—wall off
5— On—area—right
6— Gap—area—post
7— Gap—post—lead
(7 man will call "on", "short")
8— Lead—backer—influence—block left

Backfield Coaching Points:

QB— Reverse pivot—hand off—bootleg right
LH— Influence 1st man on or outside of 8 man—wall off
RH— Carrier: Run directly for hole
FB— Head for tail of 7 man—block 1st man outside of 7 man

Play #25—"182 Down"
Variation: "142 Down"

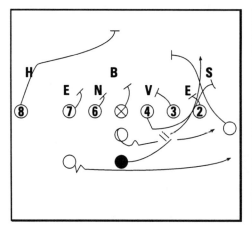
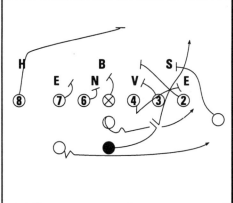

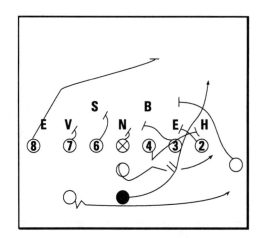

Blocking Rules:

2— Gap–down–backer
3— Gap–down–backer
4— Pull–block out
5— Reach–on–backer
6— Reach–on–backer
7— Reach–on–backer
8— Out cut

Backfield Coaching Points:

QB— Reverse pivot–hand off to FB–fake option
LH— Leave in one step motion–fake pitch
RH— Influence 1st man on or outside of 2 man–block area
FB— Carrier: Run for inside foot of 2 man

Play #26—"988 Down"
Variation: "948 Down"

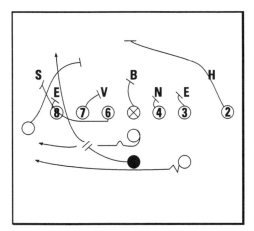
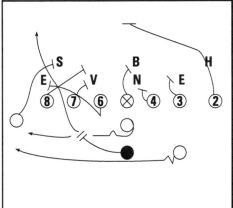

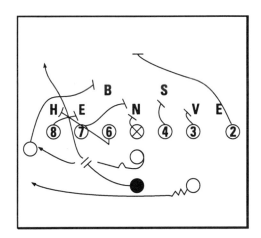

Blocking Rules:
2— Gap—out—cut
3— Reach—on—backer
4— Reach—on—backer
5— Reach—on—backer
6— Pull—block out
7— Gap—down—backer
8— Down—backer

Backfield Coaching Points:
QB— Reverse pivot—hand off to FB—fake
       option
LH— Influence 1st man or outside of 8 man—
       block area
RH— Leave in one step motion—fake pitch
FB— Carrier: Run for inside foot of 8 man

Play #27—"122 Gut"

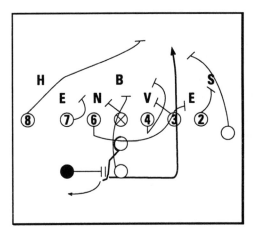
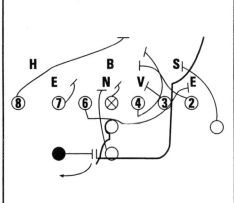
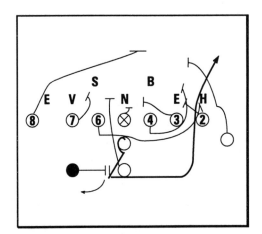

Blocking Rules:

2— Down—backer
(outside release vs. bump)
3— Gap—down—backer
4— Pull—gut
5— Reach—left
6— Pull—inside out
7— Pull—check
8— Cut off

Backfield Coaching Points:

QB—Reverse pivot—hand off to LH—bootleg
left
LH— Carrier: Receive ball—cut inside of 6
man's block
RH— Influence 1st man on or outside of 2
man—wall off
FB— Fake 21

Play #28—"928 Gut"

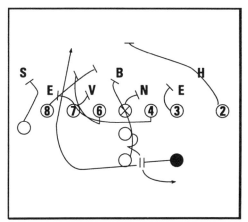

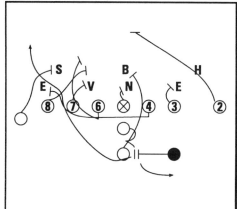

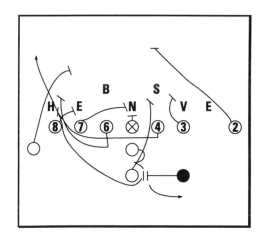

Blocking Rules:

2— Cut off
3— Pull—check
4— Pull—inside out
5— Reach—right
6— Pull—gut
7— Gap—down—backer
8— Down—backer
    (outside release vs. bump)

Backfield Coaching Points:

QB— Reverse pivot—hand off to RH—bootleg right
LH— Influence 1st man on or outside of 8 man—wall off
RH— Carrier: Receive handoff—cut inside of 4 man's block
FB— Fake 29

Play #29—"Spread 932 Counter Criss Cross"

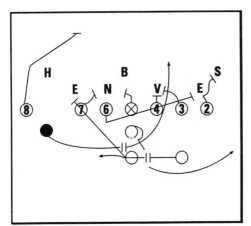
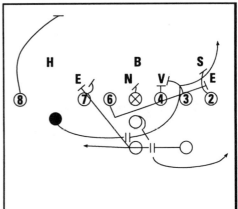

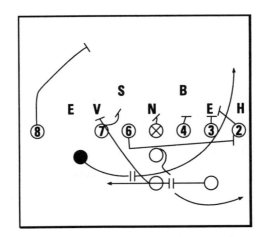

Blocking Rules:
2— Lead—backer—influence—block right
3— Gap—post—lead
4— Gap—area—post
5— On—area—left
6— Pull—inside out
7— Pull—check (pull—wall off without TE)
8— Tight: Pull—wall off
    Spread or slot: Cut off

Backfield Coaching Points:
QB— Reverse pivot—hand off to RH—bootleg right
LH— Carrier: Receive hand off from RH—head for tail of 3 man
RH— Receive hand off from QB—give ball inside to LH—fake at 39
FB— Dive for outside foot of 7 man—block 1st man off 8 man's tail

Play #30—"Spread 138 Counter Criss Cross"

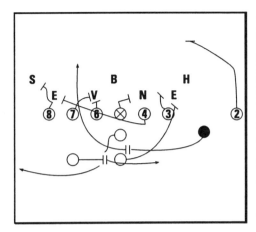
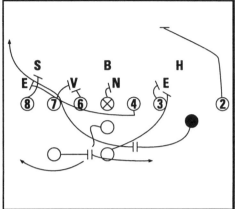

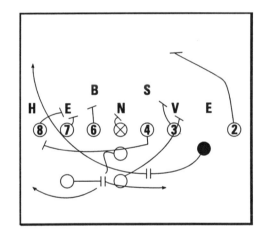

Blocking Rules:

2— Tight: Pull—wall off
   Spread or slot: Cut off
3— Pull—check (pull—wall off without TE)
4— Pull—inside out
5— On—area—right
6— Gap—area—post
7— Gap—post—lead
8— Lead—backer—influence—block left

Backfield Coaching Points:

QB— Reverse pivot—hand off to LH—bootleg left
LH— Receive hand off from QB—give ball inside to RH—fake at 31
RH— Carrier: Receive hand off from LH—head for tail of 7 man
FB— Dive for outside foot of 3 man—block 1st man off 2 man tail

Play #31—"Spread 143 On"
Variation: "Spread 143 Gut"

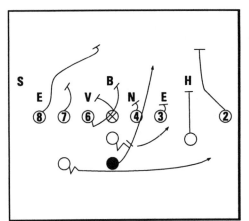

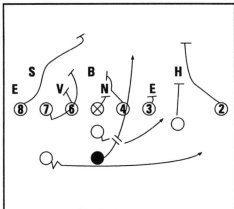

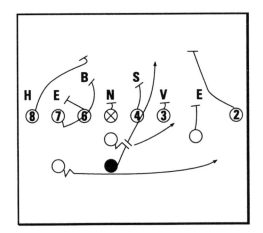

Blocking Rules:

2— Fake crack—cut off
  Tight: Gap—on—backer
3— Gap—on—backer
4— Gap—on—backer (chip vs. shade)
5— On—left
6— Pull—wall off tail of 5 man
  (odd block vs. 55)
7— Reach—on—backer (odd block vs. 55)
8— Cut off

Backfield Coaching Points:

QB— Step back—hand ball off to FB—fake 41
  Option
LH— Leave in one step motion—fake 41
  Option
RH— Block first LB from on
FB— Carrier: Clear the outside hip of 4 man—
  read defensive tackle (nose vs. 55)—
  select opening

Play #32—"Spread 947 On"
Variation: "Spread 947 Gut"

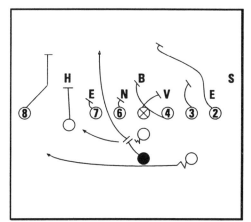

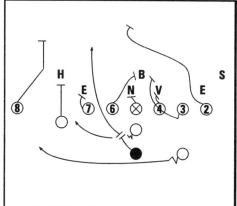

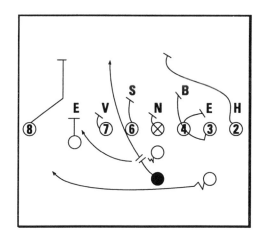

Blocking Rules:

2— Cut off
3— Reach—on—backer (odd block vs. 55)
4— Pull—wall off tail of 5 man (odd block vs. 55)
5— On—right
6— Gap—on—backer (chip vs. shade)
7— Gap—on—backer
8— Fake crack—cut off
  Tight: Gap—on—backer

Backfield Coaching Points:

QB— Step back—hand ball off to FB—fake 49 Option
LH— Block first LB from on
RH— Leave in one step motion—fake 49 Option
FB— Carrier: Clear the outside hip of 6 man—read defensive tackle (nose vs. 55)—elect opening

Play #33—"983"
Variations: "983 On"; "Reach"; "983 Gut Release"

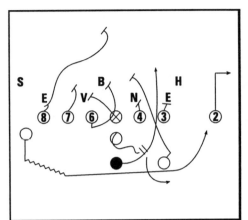
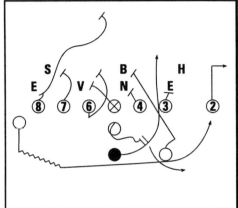

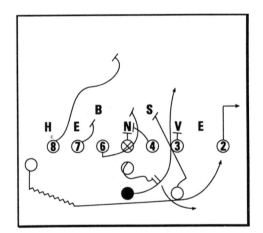

Blocking Rules:

2— Tight: On—outside—backer
    Split: Out cut
    Spread: Out cut
3— On—outside gap—backer
4— Gap—on—lead
5— Post—lead
6— Pull—block through the hole
7— Pull—check
8— Cut off

(cross block vs. single gap)

Backfield Coaching Points:

QB— Reverse pivot—ride ball to FB—fake 81
    Keep Pass
LH— Leave in early motion—fake 81 Keep
    Pass
RH— Step up 45 degrees—read tackle—block
    first backer from 5 man (double gap—
    block 3-4 seam)
FB— Carrier: Lead step—bend path for inside
    foot of 3 man—read defensive tackle—
    select opening

Play #34—"187"
Variations: "187 On"; "Reach"; "187 Gut Release"

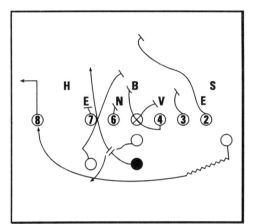
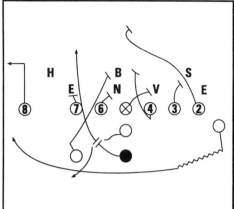

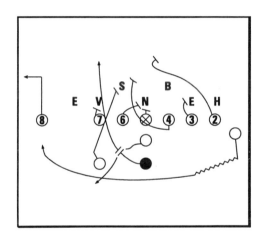

Blocking Rules:

2— Cut off
3— Pull—check
4— Pull—block through the hole
5— Post—right
6— Gap—on—lead
7— On—outside gap—backer
8— Tight: On—outside—backer
   Split: Out cut
   Spread: Out cut

Backfield Coaching Points:

QB— Reverse pivot—ride ball to FB—fake 89 Keep Pass
LH— Step up 45 degrees—read tackle—block 1st backer from 5 man (double gap—block 6-7 seam)
RH— Leave in early motion—fake 89 Keep Pass
FB— Carrier: Lead step—bend path for inside foot of 7 man—read defensive tackle—select opening

Play #35—"983 Cross Block"

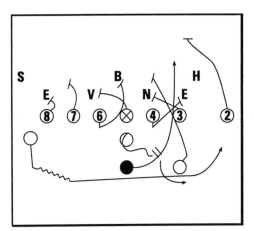 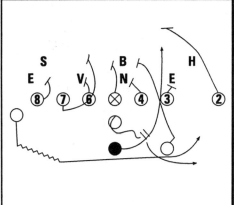

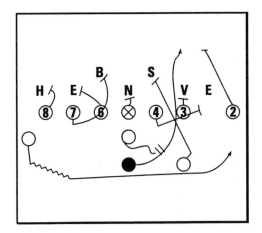

Blocking Rules:

2— Tight: Backer
   Split: Fake crack back—backer
   Spread: Cut off
3— Gap—down—on
4— Gap—pull—block out (gap call)
5— On—left
6— Pull—wall off tail of 5 man
   (odd block vs. 55)
7— Gap—on—outside (odd block vs. 55)
8— Gap—on—inside

Backfield Coaching Points:

QB— Reverse pivot—ride ball to FB—fake 81
   Keep Pass
LH— Leave in early motion—fake 81 Keep
   Pass
RH— Step up 45 degrees—dive for 3 man's
   tail—block 1st backer from 5 man
FB— Carrier: Lead step—bend path for inside
   foot of 3 man—read defensive tackle
   (nose vs. 55)—select opening

Play #36—"187 Cross Block"

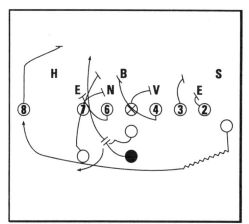
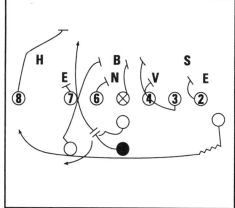

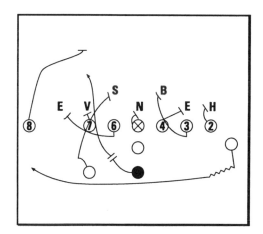

Blocking Rules:

2— Gap—on—outside
3— Gap—on—outside (odd block vs. 55)
4— Pull—wall off tail of 5 man
   (odd block vs. 55)
5— On—right
6— Gap—pull—block out (Gap call)
7— Gap—down—on
8— Tight: Backer
   Split: Fake crack back—backer
   Spread: Cut off

Backfield Coaching Points:

QB— Reverse pivot—ride ball to FB—fake 89
   Keep Pass
LH— Step up 45 degrees—dive for 7 man's
   tail—block 1st backer from 5 man
RH— Leave in early motion—fake 89 Keep
   Pass
FB— Carrier: Lead step—bend path for inside
   foot of 7 man—read defensive tackle
   (nose vs. 55)—select opening

Play #37—"Spread 123 Guard Trap"

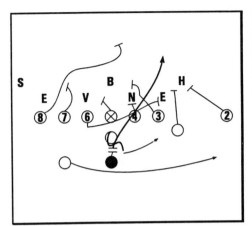

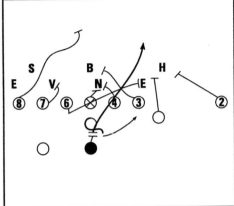

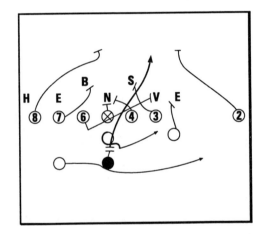

Blocking Rules:

2— Tight: Backer—outside vs. bump
   Spread (split or slot): Crack
3— Bump—lead—backer
   (with TE: lead—backer—bump)
4— Gap—on—lead—backer
5— Post—area—left (conditional post)
6— Pull—inside out
7— Gap—backer—on
8— Cut off

Backfield Coaching Points:

QB— Reverse pivot—hand off to FB—fake 21
   Trap Option
LH— Fake 21 Trap Option
RH— Block 1st LB from on
FB— Carrier: Dive for right foot of 5 man

Play #38—"Spread 927 Guard Trap"

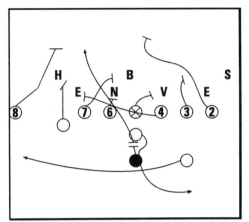

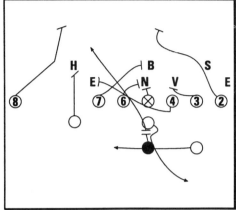

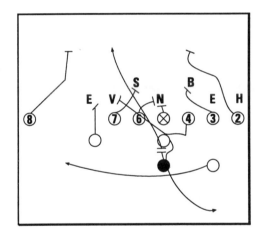

Blocking Rules:

2— Cut off
3— Gap—backer—on
4— Pull—inside out
5— Post—area—right (conditional post)
6— Gap—on—lead—backer
7— Bump—lead—backer (with TE: lead—backer—bump)
8— Tight: Backer—outside vs. bump
   Spread (split or slot): Crack

Backfield Coaching Points:

QB— Reverse pivot—hand off to FB—fake 29
   Trap Option
LH— Fake 29 Trap Option
RH— Block 1st LB from on
FB— Carrier: Dive for left foot of 5 man

Play #39—"Split 933 Counter Criss Cross"

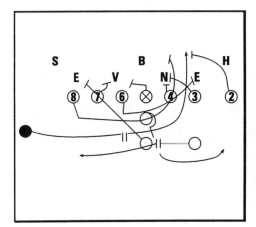
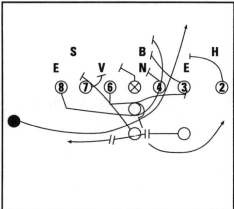

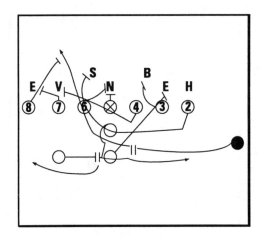

Blocking Rules:

2— Split: Wall off
 Spread: Cut off
3— Gap—lead—influence—block right
 (gap stack—backer)
4— Gap—post—lead
5— Post—area—left
6— Pull—block inside out
7— Pull—check
8— Pull—block through hole—wall off

Backfield Coaching Points:

QB— Reverse pivot—hand off to RH—bootleg
 at right
LH— Carrier: Receive hand off from RH—head
 for tail of 4 man
RH— Receive hand off from QB—give ball
 inside to LH fake at 39
FB— Dive for outside foot of 7 man—block
 1st man off 8 man's tail

Play #40—"Split 137 Counter Criss Cross"

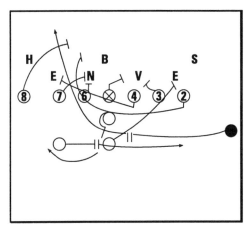
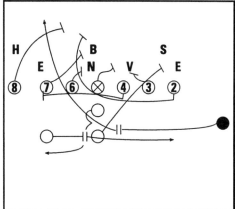

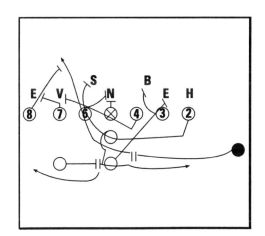

Blocking Rules:

2— Pull–block through hole–wall off
3— Pull–check
4— Pull–block inside out
5— Post–area–right
6— Gap–post–lead
7— Gap–lead–influence–block left
(gap stack–backer)
8— Split: Wall off
Spread: Cut off

Backfield Coaching Points:

QB— Reverse pivot–hand off to LH–bootleg
at left
LH— Receive handoff from QB–give ball
inside to RH–fake at 31
RH— Carrier: Receive hand off from LH–head
for tail of 6 man
FB— Dive for outside foot of 3 man–block
1st man off 2 man's tail

Play #41—"Spread 163 Draw"

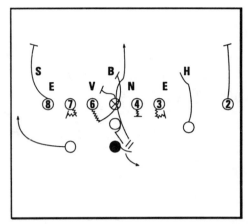
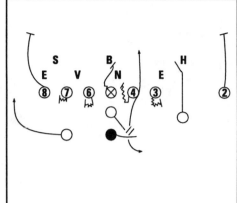

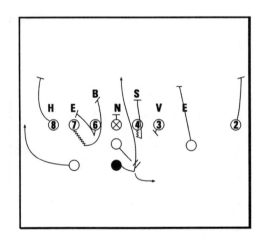

Blocking Rules:

2— Release—block down field
3— Gap—on—outside
4— Gap—on—delayed backer
5— On—left
6— Fake pass protection—gut (odd block vs. 55)
7— On—outside (odd block vs. 55)
8— Release—block down field

Backfield Coaching Points:

QB— Drop back behind 4 man—give ball to FB—continue fake
LH— Flare
RH— Release—block down field
FB— Carrier: Step to side of play—accept ball from QB—read front

Play #42—"Spread 967 Draw"

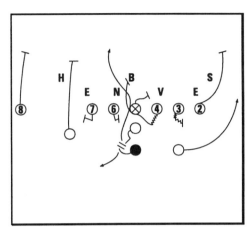 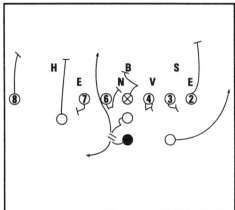

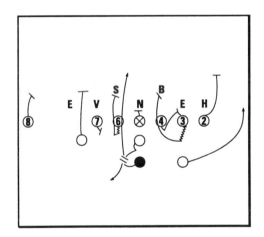

Blocking Rules:

2— Release—block down field
3— On—outside (odd block vs. 55)
4— Fake pass protection—gut (odd block vs. 55)
5— On—right
6— Gap—on—delayed backer
7— Gap—on—outside
8— Release—block down field

Backfield Coaching Points:

QB— Drop back behind 6 man—give ball to FB—continue fake
LH— Release—block down field
RH— Flare
FB— Carrier: Step to side of play—accept ball from QB—read front

CHAPTER 3

INSIDE PLAYS

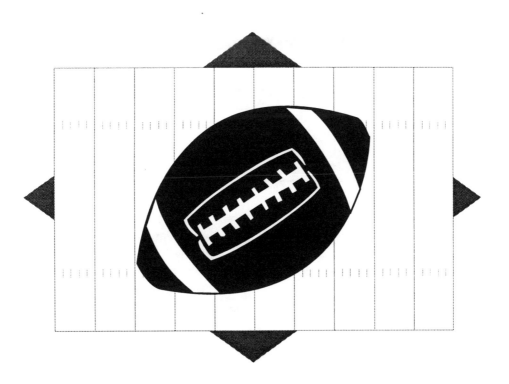

Play #43—"Spread 989 Sally at 3"

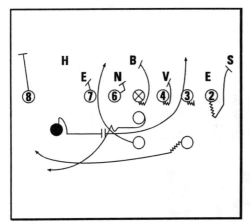
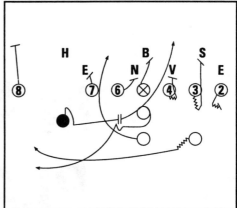
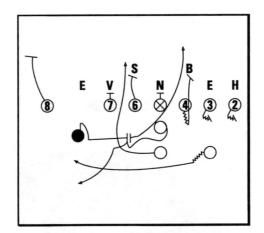

Blocking Rules:

2— Step and cup—block on—outside—delayed backer

3— Step and cup—block on—outside—delayed backer

4— Step and cup—block on—outside—delayed backer

5— Step and cup—block on—outside—delayed backer

6— Gap—on—backer

7— Gap—on—backer

8— Release
Tight: Gap—on—backer

Backfield Coaching Points:

QB— Reverse Pivot—fake ball to FB—hand off to LH

LH— Carrier: Counter step—receive ball from QB—head for tail of 4 man

RH— Leave in early motion—fake 89 Keep Pass

FB— Fake 87

Play #44—"Spread 181 Sally at 7"

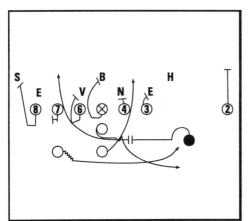

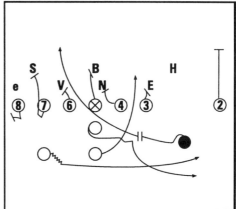

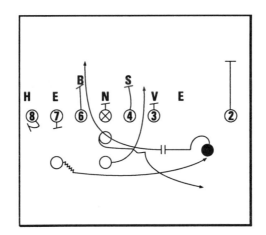

Blocking Rules:

2— Release
   Tight: Gap—on—Backer
3— Gap—on—backer
4— Gap—on—backer
5— Step and cup—block on—outside—
   delayed—backer
6— Step and cup—block on—outside—
   delayed—backer
7— Step and cup—block on—outside—
   delayed—backer
8— Step and cup—block on—outside—
   delayed—backer

Backfield Coaching Points:

QB— Reverse pivot—fake ball to FB—hand
   off to RH
LH— Leave in early motion—fake 81 Keep
   Pass
RH— Carrier: Counter step—receive ball from
   QB—head for tail of 6 man
FB— Fake 83

Play #45—"Spread 936 Counter Deuce"

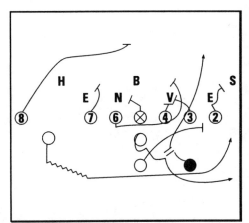
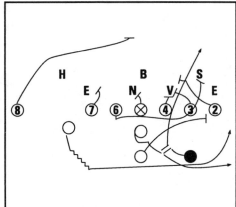
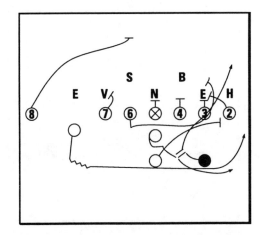

Blocking Rules:

2— Lead—backer—influence—block right
3— Gap—post—lead (3 man will call "on", "short")
4— Gap—area—post
5— On—area—post
6— Pull—wall off
7— Pull—check
8— Cut off

Backfield Coaching Points:

QB— Reverse pivot—hand ball off to RH— bootleg left
LH— Leave in early motion—block 1st man outside of 2 man
RH— Carrier: Rock weight on right foot— receive inside hand off
FB— Head for tail of 3 man—block 1st man outside of 3 man

Play #46—"Spread 134 Counter At 8"

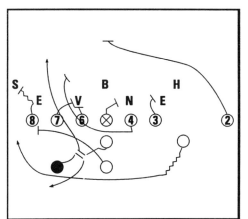

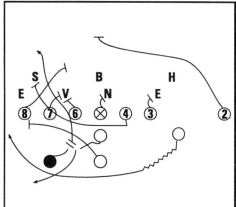

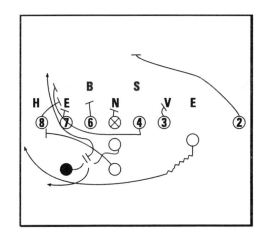

Blocking Rules:
2— Cut off
3— Pull—check
4— Pull—wall off
5— On—area—right
6— Gap—area—post
7— Gap—post—lead
   (7 man will call "on", "short")
8— Lead—backer—influence block left

Backfield Coaching Points:
QB—Reverse pivot—hand ball off to LH—
   bootleg right
LH— Carrier: Rock weight on left foot—
   receive inside handoff
RH— Leave in early motion—block 1st man
   outside of 8 man
FB— Head for tail of 7 man—block 1st man
   outside of 7 man

Play #47— "134 Counter"
Variations: "134 Counter Gut"; "184 Counter"

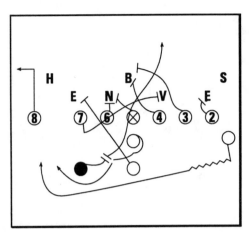
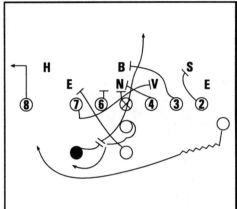

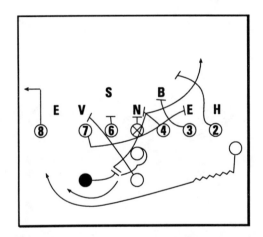

Blocking Rules:
2— Gap—backer
3— First backer from 5 man block safety
4— Gap—lead—backer (influence)
5— Post—lead—backer
6— Area-post
7— Pull—inside out
8— Spread: Out cut
   Tight: Cut off (go inside 3)

Backfield Coaching Points:
QB— Reverse pivot—hand ball off to LH—
   bootleg at left
LH— Carrier: Rock weight on left foot—
   receive inside hand off
RH— Leave in early motion—block 1st man
   outside of 8 man
FB— Drive for 6-7 seam—block 1st man in
   area

Play #48—"936 Counter"
Variation: "936 Counter Gut"

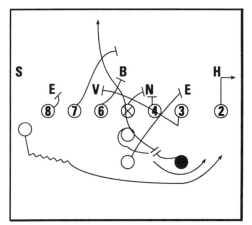

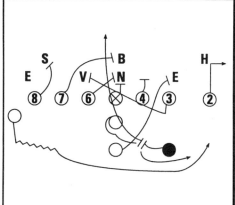

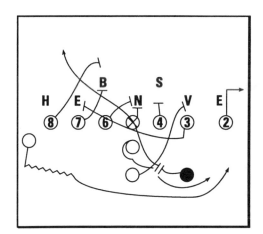

Blocking Rules:
2— Spread: Out cut
   Tight: Cut off (go inside of 3)
3— Pull—inside out
4— Area—post
5— Post—lead—backer
6— Gap—lead—backer
7— First backer from 5 man block safety
8— Gap—backer

Backfield Coaching Points:
QB—Reverse pivot—hand ball off to RH—
   bootleg at right
LH— Leave in early motion—block first man
   outside of 2 man
RH— Carrier: Rock weight on right foot—
   receive inside hand off
FB— Dive for 3-4 seam—block first man in
   area

Play #49—"Spread 134 Counter Short"

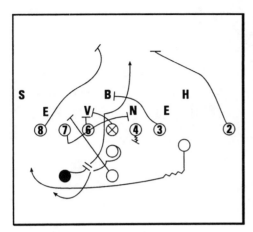
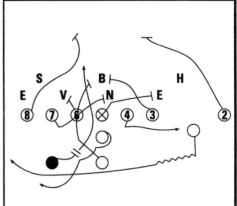

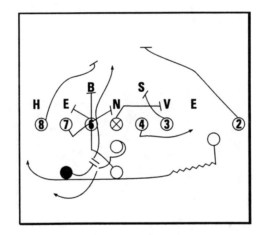

Blocking Rules:

2— Cut off
3— Backer
4— Pull away
5— Reach—release down L.O.S.
6— Outside
7— Pull—inside out (nose vs. 55)
8— Cut off

With even spacing run normal counter or counter at 8

Backfield Coaching Points:

QB— Reverse pivot—hand ball off to LH—bootleg at right
LH— Carrier: Rock weight on left foot—receive inside handoff
RH— Leave in early motion—block first man outside of 8 man
FB— Drive for 6-7 seam—block first man in area (backer vs. 55)

Play #50—"Spread 936 Counter Short"

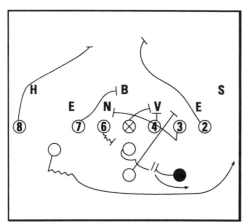

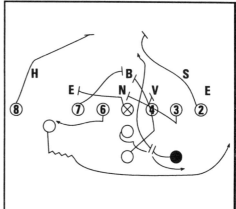

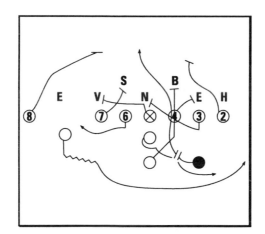

Blocking Rules:

2— Cut off
3— Pull—inside out (nose vs. 55)
4— Outside
5— Fire—release to backer
6— Pull away
7— On—backer
8— Cut off

With even spacing run normal counter
or counter at 2

Backfield Coaching Points:

QB— Reverse pivot—hand ball off to RH—
bootleg left
LH— Leave in early motion—block first man
outside of 2 man
RH— Carrier: Rock weight on right foot—
receive inside hand off
FB— Drive for 3-4 seam—block first man in
area (backer vs. 55)

Play #51—"124"
Variation: "124 On"

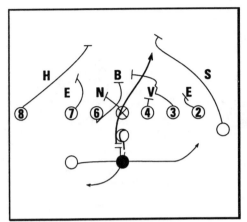

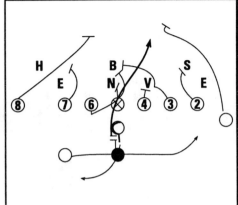

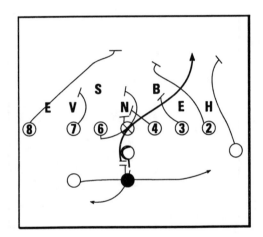

Blocking Rules:

2— Tight: Gap—cut—off
   Spread: Out cut
3— Gap—on—backer
4— Gap—on—lead
5— Post—left
6— Pull—block through hole
7— Gap—backer—on
8— Gap—cut off

Backfield Coaching Points:

QB— Reverse pivot—hand off to FB—bootleg
   left
LH— Fake 21
RH— Fake 21—cut off
FB— Carrier: Dive for left foot of 5 man

Play #52—"926"
Variation: "926 On"

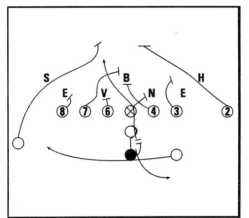
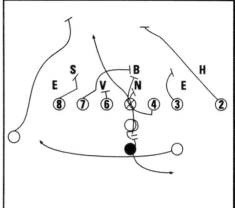

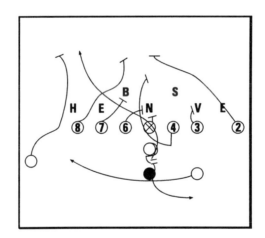

Blocking Rules:

2— Gap—cut off
3— Gap—backer—on
4— Pull—block through hole
5— Post—right
6— Gap—on—lead
7— Gap—on—backer
8— Spread: Out cut
    Tight: Gap—cut off

Backfield Coaching Points:

QB—Reverse pivot—hand off to FB—bootleg
    right
LH— Fake 29—cut off
RH— Fake 29
FB— Carrier: Dive for right foot of 5 man

Play #53—"124 Guard Trap"

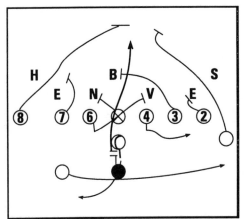
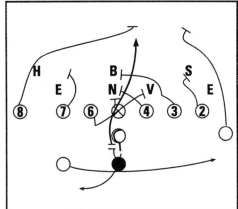
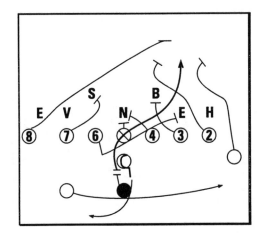

Blocking Rules:

2— Spread: Out cut
    Tight: Gap—cut off
3— 1st backer from 5 man
4— Gap—lead—backer—influence
5— Post—left
6— Pull—inside out
7— Gap—backer—on
    Spread: Cut off
8— Gap—cut off

Backfield Coaching Points:

QB—Reverse pivot—hand off to FB—bootleg
    left
LH— Fake 21
RH— Fake 21—cut off
FB— Carrier: Dive for left foot of 5 man

Play #54—"926 Guard Trap"

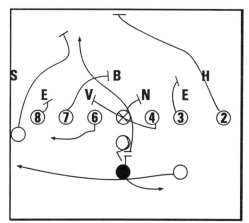
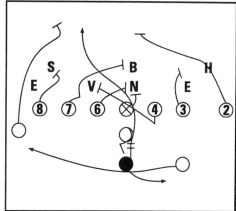

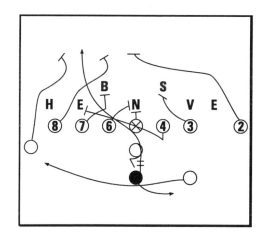

Blocking Rules:

2— Gap—cut off
3— Gap—backer—on
4— Pull—inside out
5— Post—right
6— Gap—lead—backer—influence
7— 1st backer from 5 man
8— Spread: Out cut
    Tight: Gap—cut off

Backfield Coaching Points:

QB— Reverse pivot—hand off to FB—bootleg
    left
LH— Fake 29
RH— Fake 29
FB— Carrier: Dive for right foot of 5 man

Play #55—"924 Gut"

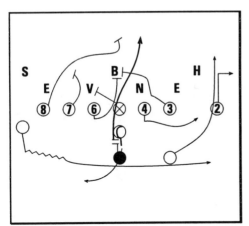
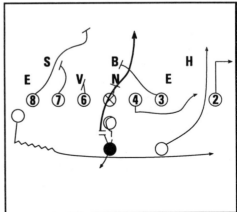
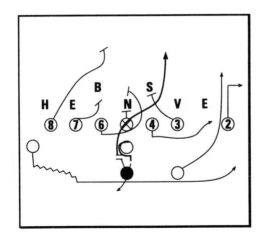

Blocking Rules:

2— Spread: Out cut
    Tight: Gap—backer—cut off
3— 1st backer from 5 man
4— Pull—fake 21
5— On—left
6— Pull—block through the hole
7— Gap—backer—on
8— Gap—cut off

Backfield Coaching Points:

QB— Reverse pivot—hand off to FB—bootleg
    left
LH— Fake 21
RH— Fake 21—cut off
FB— Carrier: Dive for left foot of 5 man

Play #56—"126 Gut"

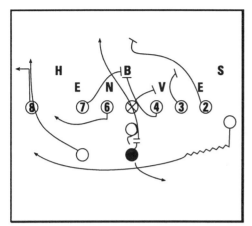
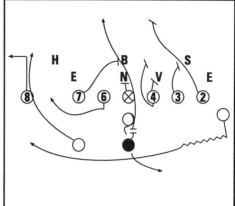

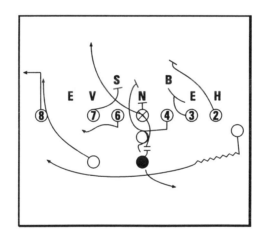

Blocking Rules:
2— Gap—cut off
3— Gap—backer—on
4— Pull—block through the hole
5— On—right
6— Pull—fake 29
7— 1st backer from 5 man
8— Spread: Out cut
    Tight: Gap—backer—cut off

Backfield Coaching Points:
QB—Reverse pivot—hand off to FB—bootleg
    right
LH— Fake 29
RH— Fake 29
FB— Carrier: Dive for right foot of 5 man

Play #57—"Tight T 944 Wedge"

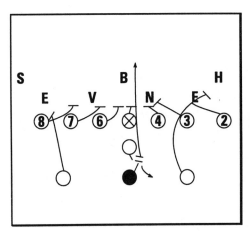

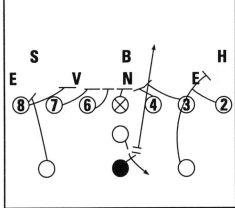

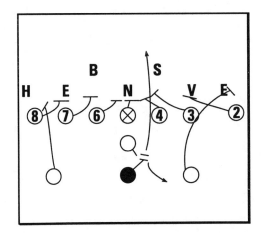

Blocking Rules:

2— Close with left foot wedging area from 3 man's shoulder

3— Close with left foot wedging area from 4 man's shoulder

4— Wedge your left shoulder—blocking area

5— Wedge your right shoulder—blocking area

6— Close with right foot wedging area with 5 man's shoulder

7— Close with right foot wedging area from 6 man's shoulder

8— Close with right foot wedging area from 7 man's shoulder

Backfield Coaching Points:

QB— Open to FB—bring ball to him quickly

LH— Shorten—block 1st man outside of 8 man's wedge

RH— Dive for tail of 3 man—block 1st man outside of 2 man's wedge

FB— Carrier: Receive ball—quickly run to line—dive or slide to opening for yardage

Play #58—"T 944 Wedge Quarterback Sneak"

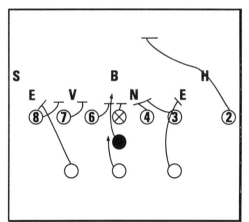

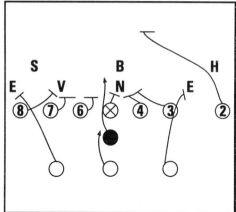

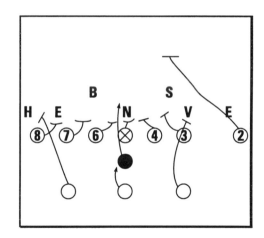

Blocking Rules:

2— Close with left foot wedging area from 3 man's shoulder

3— Close with left foot wedging area from 4 man's shoulder

4— Wedge your left shoulder—blocking area

5— Wedge your right shoulder—blocking area

6— Close with right foot wedging area with 5 man's shoulder

7— Close with right foot wedging area from 6 man's shoulder

8— Close with right foot wedging area from 7 man's shoulder

Backfield Coaching Points:

QB— Dive or slide to opening for yardage

LH— Shorten—block 1st man outside of 8 man's wedge

RH— Dive for tail of 3 man—block 1st man outside of 2 man's wedge

FB— Follow QB to hole

CHAPTER 4

PASS PLAYS

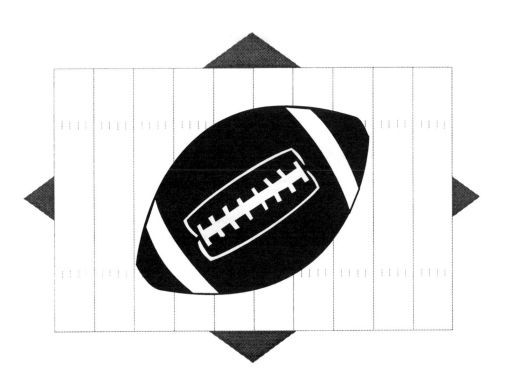

Play #59—"Blue 11"
Variation: "Blue 11 Throwback"

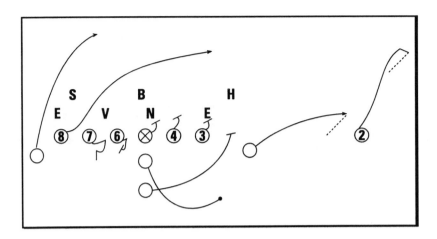

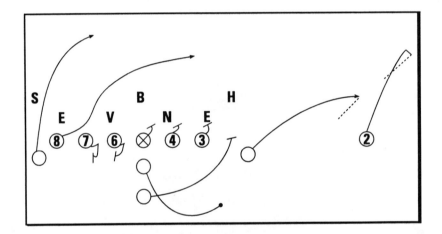

Blocking Rules:

2— Run "out" pattern at 12 yards
3— Reach—on—area
4— Reach—on—area
5— Reach and cup
6— Reach and cup
7— Reach and cup
8— Crossing pattern

Backfield Coaching Points:

QB— Sprint out right—option run or pass
LH— Soft cross
RH— Flat pattern
FB— Aggressively block first free man at flank

Play #60—"Red 19"
Variations: "Blue 19 Seam"; "119 Throwback"

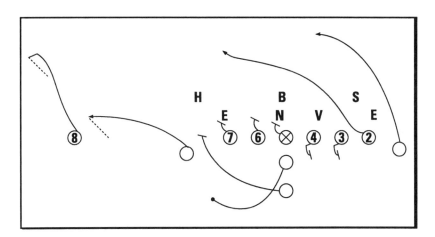

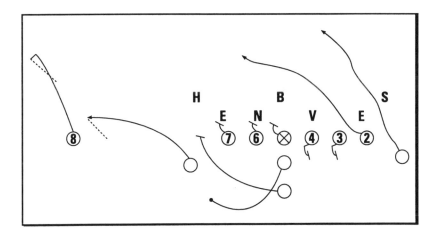

Blocking Rules:
2— Crossing pattern
3— Reach and cup
4— Reach and cup
5— Reach and cup
6— Reach—on—area
7— Reach—on—area
8— Run out pattern at 12 yards (loop in)

Backfield Coaching Points:
QB— Sprint out left—option run or pass
LH— Flat pattern
RH— Soft cross
FB— Aggressively block first free man at flank

Play #61— "Blue 51"

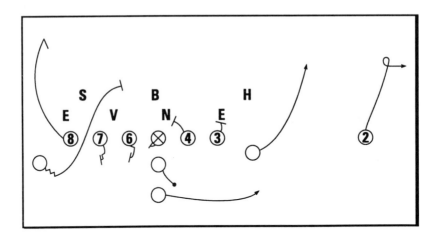

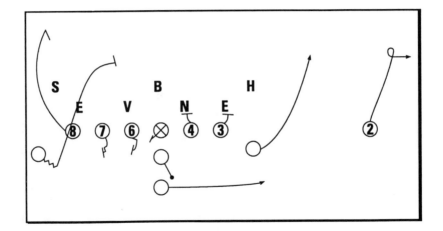

Blocking Rules:

2— Run loop "out" pattern at 6 yards (loop in vs. 200)

3— Gap—on—outside

4— Gap—on—inside

5— Step and cup

6— Step and cup

7— Step and cup

8— Hook at 12 yards by 5 yards—with a call of eagle the 5 man must block the nose man and the backside G and T must look for the LB fire—consider flaring both HB and FB vs. man

Backfield Coaching Points:

QB— Drop back right—3 steps—then to 5-7 depending on development or individual call

LH— Block first free backer—drag if B drops and hook at 5 yds in open area

RH— Turn up field and look over inside shoulder. (Hook at 12 yds.)—run companion route if pattern is called.

FB— Read inside backer—if he drops read 3— flare if he drives. Gap call—block 3

Play #62—"Red 59"

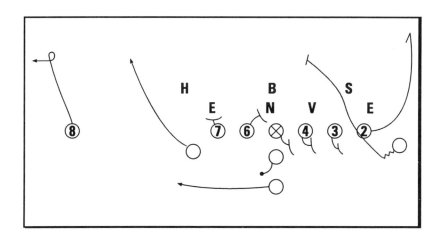

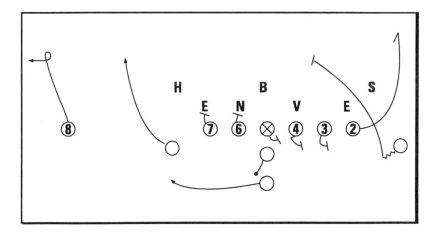

Blocking Rules:
2— Hook at 12 yds by 5 yds
3— Step and cup
4— Step and cup
5— Step and cup
6— Gap—on—inside
7— Gap—on—inside
8— Run loop "out" pattern at 6 yds (loop in vs. 200)

Backfield Coaching Points:
QB— Drop back left—3 steps—then to 5-7 depending on development or individual call. (Drop as 51 with three step drop,)
LH— Turn up field and look over inside shoulder (hook at 12 yds)—run companion route if pattern is called
RH— Block first free backer—drag if B drops and hook at 5 yds in open area
FB— Read inside backer—read 3—flare if he drives—hook if he drops. Gap call—block 3

Play #63—"Loose (Left Trips) 61"
Variations: "Loose (Right Trips) 61"; "Loose 61"

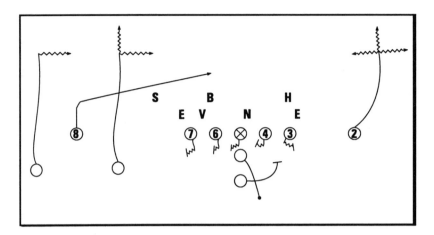

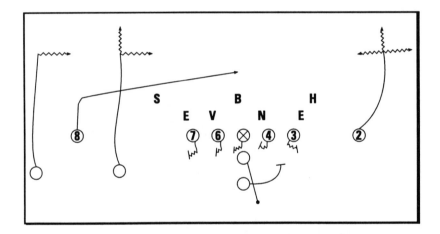

Blocking Rules:

2— Run read pattern
3— Gap—on—outside
4— Gap—on—inside
5— Step and cup
6— Step and cup
7- Step and cup
8— Run under pattern

Backfield Coaching Points:

QB— Roll right 5 steps—check front side
    then back side
LH— Run option pattern
RH— Run read pattern
FB— Read inside backer. Read 3—block if he
    drives—hook if he drops. Gap call—
    block 3.

Play #64—"Loose (Right Trips) 69"
Variations: "Loose (Left Trips) 69"; "Loose 69"

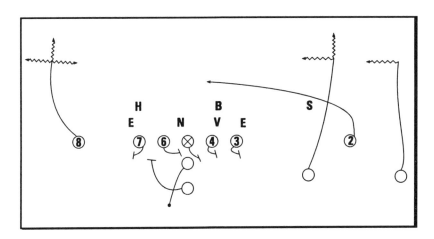

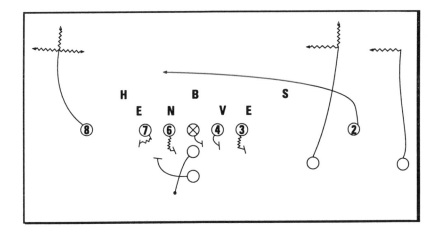

Blocking Rules:

2— Run under pattern
3— Step and cup
4— Step and cup
5— Step and cup
6— Gap—on—inside
7— Gap—on—inside
8— Run read pattern

Backfield Coaching Points:

QB— Roll right 5 steps—check front side then back side
LH— Run option pattern
RH— Run read pattern
FB— Read inside backer. Read 3—block if he drives—hook if he drops. Gap call—block 3

Play #65—"Blue 21 Waggle"

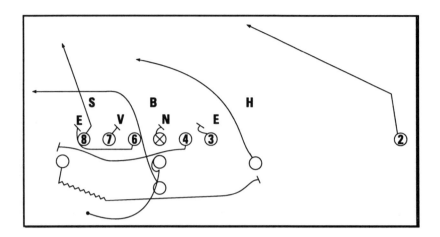

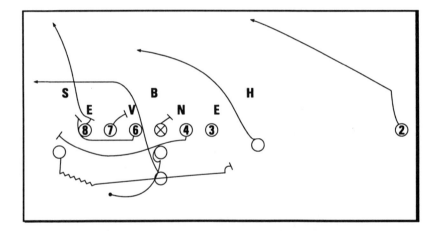

Blocking Rules:

2— Tight: Crossing pattern (read safety)
    Spread: Post pattern—key HB's pattern
3— Gap—on—area (pull—check vs. eagle)
4— Pull—read 6's block—clean up chase—
    block out (do not pull vs. eagle)
5— Reach—right
6— Pull—hook 2nd man from 5
7— Gap—down—on
8— Tight: Waggle pattern
    Spread: Fly
    Waggle out: 15 yards

Backfield Coaching Points:

QB— Reverse pivot—fake to LH—option run
    or pass
LH— Start in motion—block 1st man outside
    of 3 man's block
RH— Fake 921—key middle safety—run
    crossing pattern
FB— Dive for inside foot of 6 man—block 6
    man's area—slide delayed into flat

Play #66—"Blue 29 Waggle"

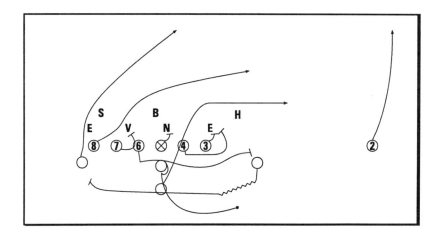

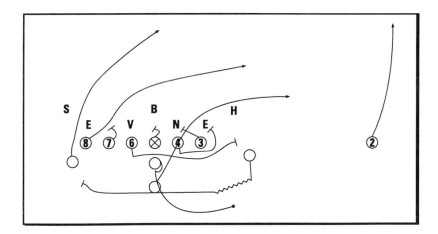

Blocking Rules:

2— Tight: Waggle pattern
   Spread: Fly
3— Gap—down—on
4— Pull—hook 2nd man from 5
5— Reach—left
6— Pull—Read 4's block—clean up chase—block out (do not pull vs. eagle)
7— Gap—on—area (pull—check vs. eagle)
8— Tight: Crossing pattern (read safety)
   Spread: Post pattern—key HB's pattern

Backfield Coaching Points:

QB— Reverse pivot—fake to RH—option run or pass
LH— Fake 129—key middle safety—run crossing pattern
RH— Start in motion—block 1st man outside of 7 man's block
FB— Dive for inside foot of 4 man—block 4 man's area—slide delayed into flat

Play #67—"Red 21 Waggle Solid"

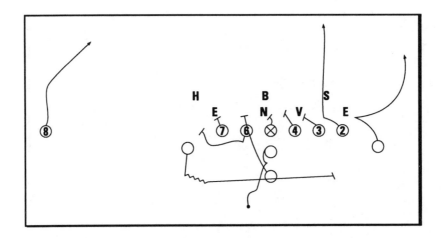

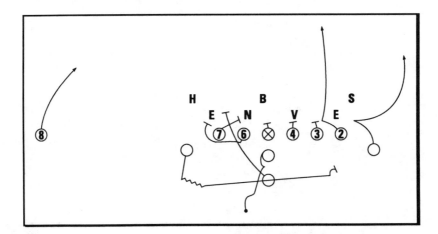

Blocking Rules:

2— Fake 21—release through inside shoulder of safety
3— Gap—on—area
4— Gap—on—area (pull vs. even defense)
5— Reach—right
6— Gap—on—pull
7— Gap—on—outside
8— Waggle pattern

Backfield Coaching Points:

QB— Reverse pivot—fake to LH—begin waggle path—set up on inside foot of 7 man at a depth of 7 yds
LH— Fake 21—block 3rd man—flare
RH— Fake 21—run fly pattern
FB— Dive for left foot of 5 man block backer

Play #68—"Blue 29 Waggle Solid"

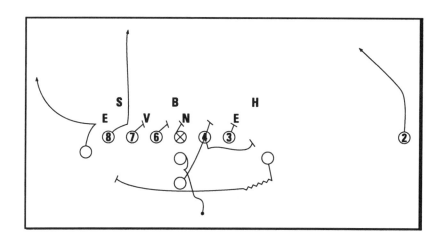

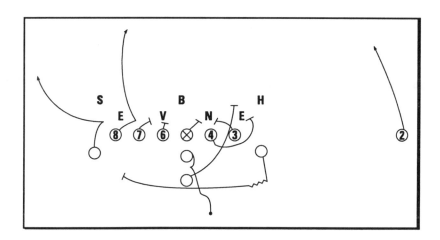

Blocking Rules:

2— Waggle pattern
3— Gap—on—outside
4— Gap—on—pull
5— Reach—left
6— Gap—on—area (pull vs. even defense)
7— Gap—on—area
8— Fake 21—release through inside shoulder of safety

Backfield Coaching Points:

QB—Reverse pivot—fake to RH—begin waggle path—set up on inside foot of 3 man at a depth of 7 yds
LH— Fake 29—run fly pattern
RH— Fake 29—block 3rd man—flare
FB— Dive for right foot of 5 man—block backer

Play #69—"Red 81 Keep Pass"

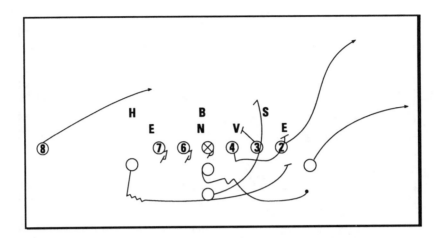

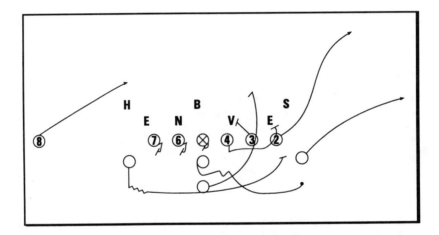

Blocking Rules:

2— Tight: Seam (inside release vs. 55)
   Spread: Out at 15 yds
3— Gap—down—area (with called pattern: Gap—on—inside)
4— Gap—pull—log 1st man on or outside of 3 man (with called pattern: Gap—on—inside)
5— Step and cup
6— Step and cup
7— Step and cup
8— Tight: Step and cup—drag
   Spread: Crossing

Backfield Coaching Points:

QB— Reverse pivot—ride ball to FB—option run or pass
LH— One step motion—get in front of QB—block 1st man off corner
RH— Sprint to flat (look immediately)—flare from dive position
FB— Straighten path for outside foot of 3 man—block 1st man in area. When individual pattern is called use 83 technique. Hook at 5 yds with called pattern.

Play #70—"Red 89 Keep Pass"
Variation: "Spread 989 Keep Pass (called pattern)"

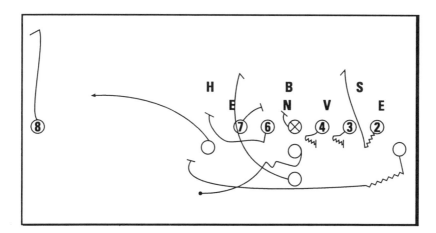

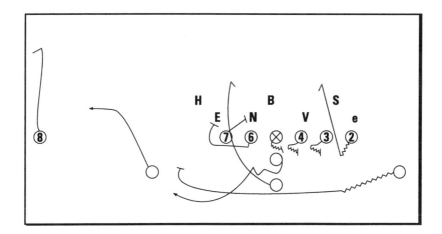

Blocking Rules:

2— Tight: Step and cup—drag
   Spread: Crossing
3— Step and cup
4— Step and cup
5— Step and cup
6— Gap—pull—log 1st man on or outside of
   7 man (with called pattern: Gap—on—
   inside)
7— Gap—down—area (with called pattern:
   Gap—on—outside)
8— Tight: Seam (inside release vs. 55)
   Spread: Out at 15 yds

Backfield Coaching Points:

QB— Reverse pivot—ride ball to FB—option
   run or pass
LH— Sprint to flat (look immediately)—flare
   from dive position
RH— One step motion—get in front of QB—
   block 1st man off corner
FB— Straighten path for outside foot of 7
   man—block 1st man in area. When
   individual pattern is called use 87
   technique. Hook at 5 yds with called
   pattern.

Play #71—"Blue 81 Waggle"

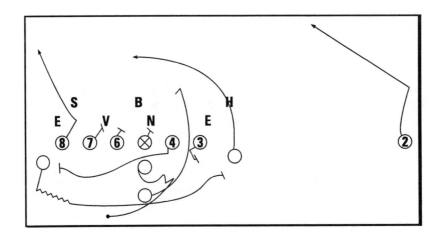

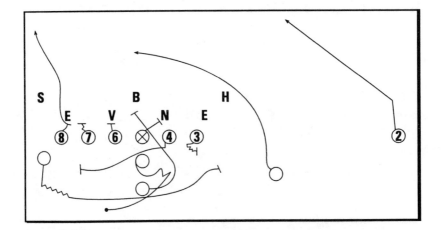

Blocking Rules:

2— Tight: Crossing pattern
   Spread: Post pattern
3— Step and cup
4— Pull (get depth)—block 1st man outside
   of 7 man's block
5— On—right—eagle call block right
6— Gap—on—inside—eagle call block right
7— Gap—on—outside
8— Waggle pattern

Backfield Coaching Points:

QB— Reverse pivot—on midline—place ball on
   hip—get depth but do not threaten
   flank
LH— Motion—block first man outside of 3
   man's block
RH— WB: Run crossing pattern
   DB: Use Sally technique—run flat
   pattern
FB— Take one lateral step right—bend path
   to block 1st backer from 5 man

Play #72—"Red 89 Waggle"

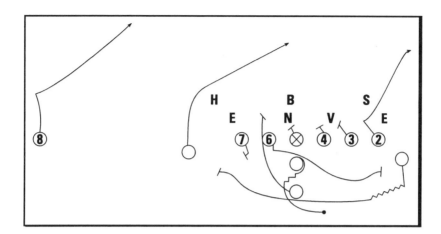

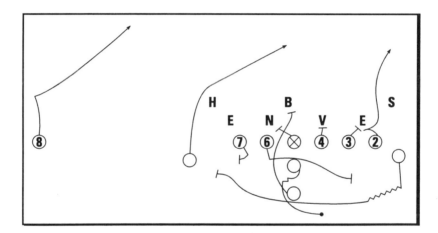

Blocking Rules:

2— Waggle pattern
3— Gap—on—inside
4— Gap—on—area—inside—eagle call block left
5— On—left—eagle call B block left
6— Pull (get depth)—block 1st man outside 3 man's block
7— Step and cup
8— Tight: Crossing
    Spread: Post

Backfield Coaching Points:

QB—Reverse pivot—on midline—place ball on hip—get depth but do not threaten flank
LH— WB: Run crossing pattern
    DB: Use Sally technique—run flat pattern
RH— Motion—block 1st man outside of 7 man's block
FB— Take one lateral step left—bend path to block 1st backer from 5 man

Play #73—"Blue 21 Trap Option Pass"

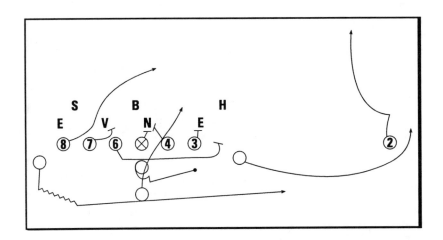

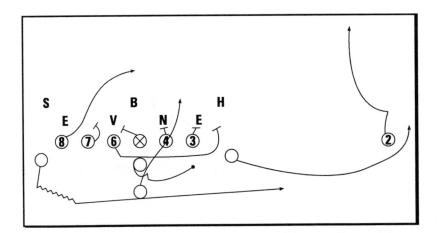

Blocking Rules:

2— Slant
3— Gap on
4— Gap—lead—down
5— Post—left
6— Pull—log 1st man outside 3 man
7— Pull—check
8— Release inside—crossing

Backfield Coaching Points:

QB—Reverse pivot to midline for 2 steps—
   read secondary—pass or option
LH— Take off on snap—run option path—look
   for pitch
RH— Flare outside slant pattern—look for
   pass over inside shoulder
RB— Fake 24 GT

Play #74—"Red 29 Trap Option Pass"
Variation: "129 Trap Option Pass"

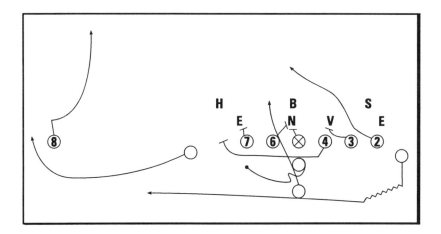

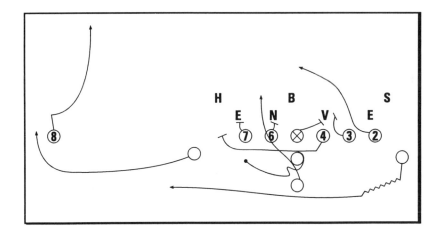

Blocking Rules:

2— Release inside—crossing
3— Pull—check
4— Pull—log first man outside 7 man
5— Post—right
6— Gap—lead—down
7— Gap—on
8— Slant

Backfield Coaching Points:

QB— Reverse pivot to midline for 2 steps— read secondary—pass or option
LH— Flare outside slant pattern—look for pass over inside shoulder
RH— Take off on snap—run option path—look for pitch

Play #75—"Blue 41 Option Pass"
Variation: "Look In"

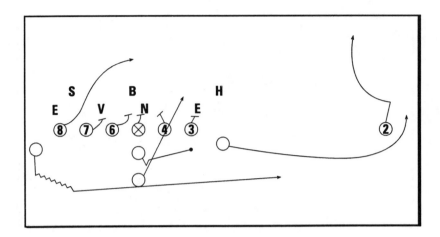

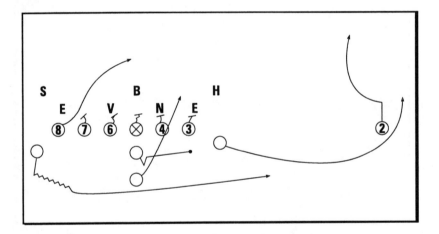

Blocking Rules:

2— Slant
3— Gap—on—area
4— Gap—on—lead
5— Post—area
6— Reach—on—area
7— Reach—on—area
8— Release inside—crossing

Backfield Coaching Points:

QB— Step back—ride ball to FB—read secondary—pass or option
LH— Leave in one step motion—be in position to receive pitch then pass.
RH— Flare outside slant pattern—block
FB— Fake 41 Option

Play #76—"Red 49 Option Pass"

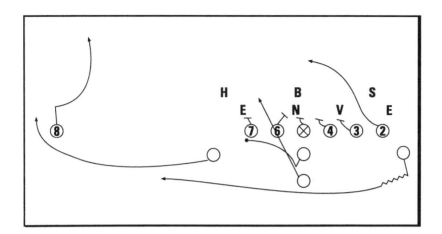

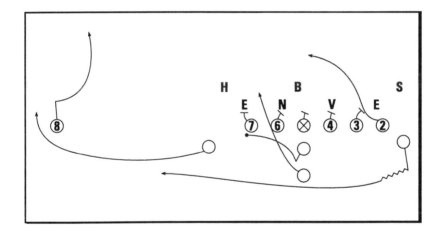

Blocking Rules:

2— Release inside—crossing
3— Reach—on—area
4— Reach—on—area
5— Post—area
6— Gap—on—lead
7— Gap—on—area
8— Slant

Backfield Coaching Points:

QB— Step back—ride ball to FB—read
     secondary—pass or option
LH— Flare outside slant pattern—block
RH— Leave in one step motion—be in position
     to receive pitch then pass
FB— Fake 49 Option

Play #77—"134 Counter Bootleg Pass"
Variation: "Spread 134 Counter B/L Opposite"

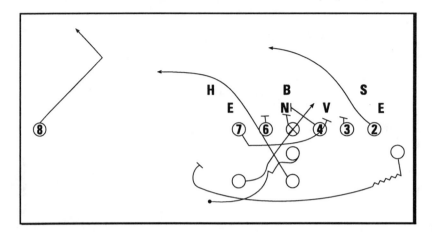

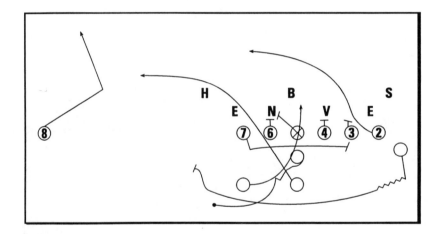

Blocking Rules:

2— Tight: Crossing pattern
   Spread: Post
3— Gap—on—area
4— Gap—on—lead
5— Post—lead
6— Area—post
7— Pull—block chase
8— Angle flag pattern—if covered sideline at no less than 15 yds

Backfield Coaching Points:

QB— Reverse pivot—fake 34 Counter—bootleg run or pass option
LH— Fake 34 Counter
RH— Leave in early motion—block 1st free man of corner
FB— Run 34 Counter—run into flat at 5 yds—block 1st man outside 6 man when opposite is called

Play #78—"936 Counter Bootleg Pass"
Variation: "Spread 936 Counter B/L Opposite"

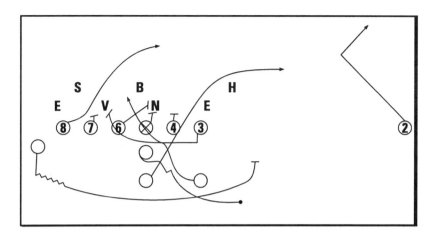

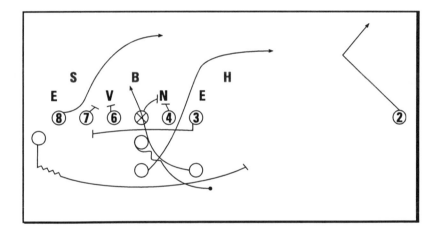

Blocking Rules:

2— Angle flag pattern—if covered sideline at no less than 15 yds
3— Pull—block chase
4— Area—post
5— Post—lead
6— Gap—on—lead
7— Gap—on—area
8— Tight: Crossing pattern
    Spread: Post

Backfield Coaching Points:

QB— Reverse pivot—fake 36 Counter—bootleg run or pass protection
LH— Leave in early motion—block first free man off corner
RH— Fake 36 Counter
FB— Run 36 Counter—run into flat at 5 yards—block first man outside 4 man when opposite is called

CHAPTER 5

SPECIAL SITUATION PLAYS

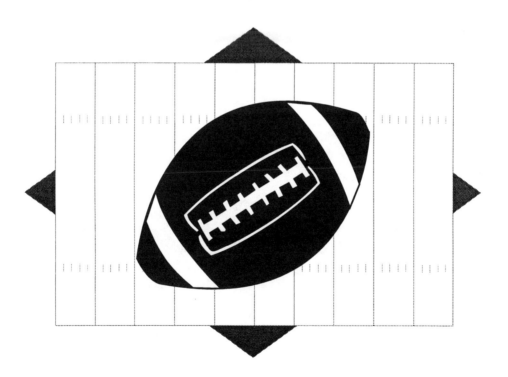

Play #79—"X 139"

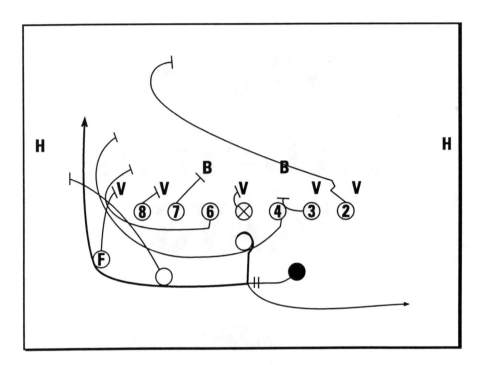

Blocking Rules:
2— Cut off
3— Block 1st man outside of 5
4— Pull—personal escort
5— On—left
6— Pull—turn up—wall off
7— Gap—inside
8— Gap—on—inside

Backfield Coaching Points:
QB—Reverse pivot—hand off—fake bootleg at one
LH— Block inside out—1st man outside at fullback's block
RH— Carrier: Leave in motion—carry at nine—use FB's block then LH's
FB— Block 1st man on or outside 8

See Play 80—"139" on page 97 for the diagrams showing other defensive spacings.

Play #80—"139"

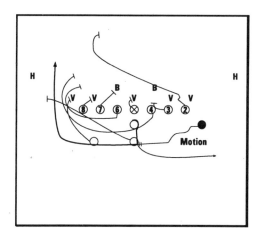

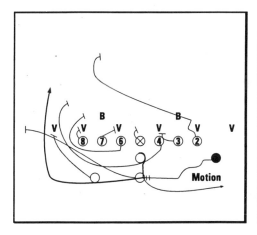
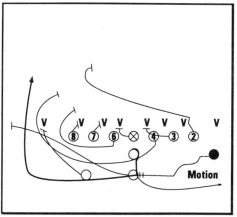

Blocking Rules:

2— Cut off
3— Block 1st man outside of 5
4— Pull—personal escort
5— On—block left
6— Pull—turn up—wall off
7— Gap—inside
8— Gap—on—inside

Backfield Coaching Points:

QB— Reverse pivot—hand off—fake bootleg at one
LH— Block outside in—1st man outside of 8
RH— Carrier: Leave in motion—carry at nine—use LH's block then FB's
FB— Block out—1st man outside of LH's block (If LH is blocking out—turn in before blocking out.)

Play #81— "Tight 139 Counter Criss Cross"

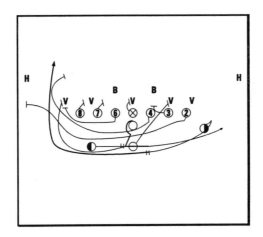

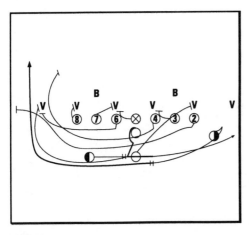
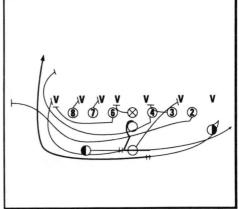

Blocking Rules:

2— Pull—block out
3— Block 2nd man on or outside of 5
4— Pull—block through and in
5— On—area—left
6— Pull—hook 1st man outside of 8's block
7— Gap—inside
8— Gap—on—inside

Backfield Coaching Points:

QB— Reverse pivot—hand ball off to LH— bootleg—block outside in
LH— Receive hand off—criss cross ball outside to RH—fake at one
RH— Carrier: Jab step with right foot— reverse for outside criss cross hand off—get depth—turn up field
FB— Check off outside foot of 3

Play #82—"Tight 239 Counter Criss Cross"

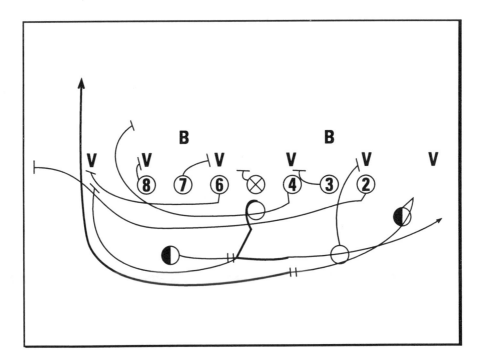

Blocking Rules:

2— Pull—block out

3— Block 2nd man on or outside of 5

4— Pull—block through and in

5— On—area—left

6— Pull—hook 1st man outside of 8's block (get quick depth)

7— Gap—inside

8— Gap—on—inside

Backfield Coaching Points:

QB— Reverse pivot—hand ball off to LH—bootleg—block outside in

LH— Receive hand off—criss cross ball outside to RH—fake at one

RH— Carrier: Jab step with right foot—reverse for outside criss cross hand off—get depth—turn up field

FB— Check off outside foot of 3

See Play 81—"139 Counter Criss Cross" on page 98 for the diagrams showing other defensive spacings.

Play #83—"Right 139 Counter Criss Cross"

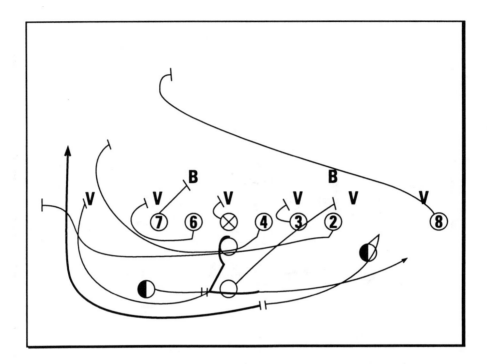

Blocking Rules:

2— Pull—block out
3— Block 2nd man on or outside of 5
4— Pull—block though and in
5— On—area—left
6— Pull—hook 1st man outside of 7's block (get quick depth)
7— Gap—inside
8— Opposite side—block—cut off

Backfield Coaching Points:

QB— Reverse pivot—hand ball off to LH—bootleg—block outside in
LH— Receive hand off—criss cross ball outside to RH—fake at one
RH— Carrier: Jab step with right foot—reverse for outside criss cross hand off—get depth—turn up field
FB— Check off outside foot of 3

Play #84—"X 139 Counter Criss Cross"

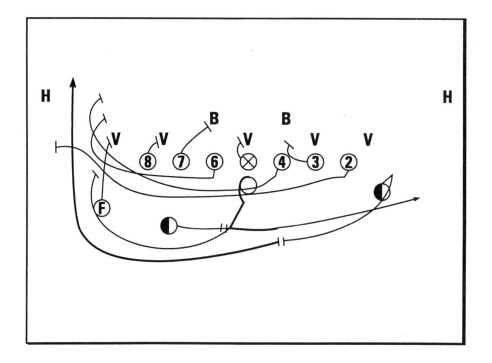

Blocking Rules:
2— Pull—block out
3— Block 2nd man on or outside of 5
4— Pull—block through and in
5— On—area—left
6— Pull—hook 1st man outside of fullback's block (get quick depth)
7— Gap—inside
8— Gap—on—inside

Backfield Coaching Points:
QB— Reverse pivot—hand ball off to LH—bootleg—block outside in
LH— Receive hand off—criss cross ball outside to RH—fake at one
RH— Carrier: Jab step with right foot—reverse for outside criss cross hand off—get depth—turn up field
FB— Block 1st man on or outside 8

Play #85—"X Right 149 Counter Criss Cross"

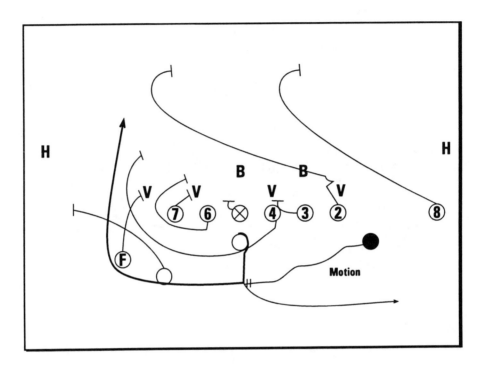

Blocking Rules:
2— Cut off
3— Block 1st man outside of 5
4— Pull—personal escort
5— On—left
6— Pull—turn up—wall off
7— Gap—inside
8— Opposite side—cut off

Backfield Coaching Points:
QB— Reverse pivot—hand off—fake bootleg
    at one
LH— Block out 1st man outside of FB's block
RH— Carrier: Leave in motion—carry at
    nine—use FB's block then LH's
FB— Block first man on or outside 7

See Play 81—"139 Counter Criss Cross" on page 98 for the diagrams showing other
defensive spacings.

Play #86—"Tight 149"

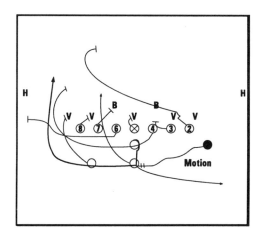

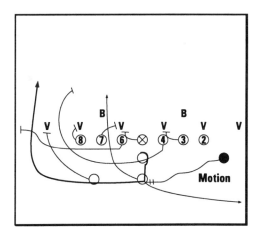
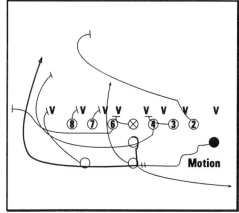

Blocking Rules:
2— Cut off
3— Block 1st man outside of 5
4— Pull—personal escort
5— On—left
6— Pull—block out on HB (adjust course to LH's block)
7— Gap—inside
8— Gap—on—inside

Backfield Coaching Points:
QB— Reverse pivot—hand off to RH—fake bootleg at one
LH— Block outside in—first man outside of 8
RH— Carrier: Leave in motion receive ball— use LH's block then 6's
FB— Drive for 7-6 seam—turn in—wall off

Play #87—"Right 229 No Motion"

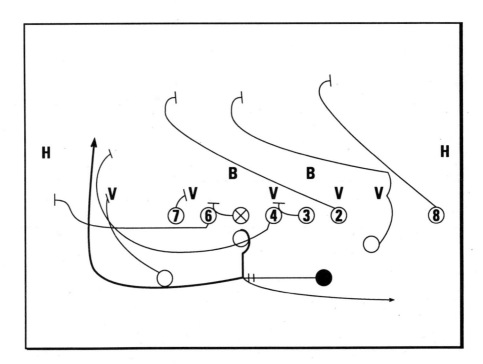

Blocking Rules:
2— Cut off
3— Cut off
4— Pull—personal escort
5— On—left
6— Pull—block out on HB (adjust course to LH's block)
7— Gap—inside
8— Opposite side—cut off

Backfield Coaching Points:
QB— Reverse pivot—hand off to FB—fake bootleg at one
LH— Block outside in—1st man outside 7
RH— Block cut off—fake block on 1st man inside
FB— Carrier: Receive ball—run at nine—use LH's block— then 6's

Play #88—"Right 231 Fan"

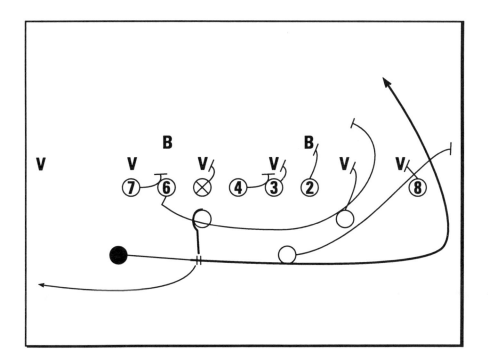

Blocking Rules:
2— Gap—on—outside
3— Gap—on—outside
4— Gap—on—inside
5— On—away
6— Pull—turn up—wall off
7— Block 2nd man on or outside of 5
8— Opposite side—block 1st man inside

Backfield Coaching Points:
QB— Reverse pivot—hand ball off to LH—
fake bootleg at nine
LH— Carrier: Receive ball—look for end's
block—turn upfield
RH— Block 2nd man on or outside of 2—use
appropriate shoulder (start at 2-3 gap)
FB— Block 1st man outside of 2's block (any
way)

See Play 89—"Split 131 Fan" on following page for the diagrams showing other defensive spacings.

Play #89—"Split 131 Fan"

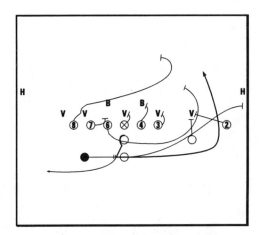

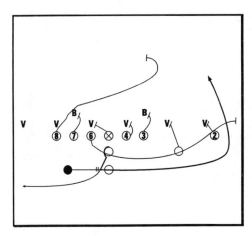
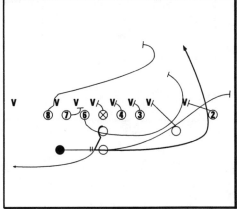

Blocking Rules:

2— Block 1st man inside
3— Gap—on—outside
4— Gap—on—inside
5— On—block left
6— Pull—turn up—wall off
7— Block 2nd man on or outside of 5
8— Cut off

Backfield Coaching Points:

QB— Reverse pivot—hand ball off to LH—
fake bootleg at nine
LH— Carrier: Receive ball—look for end's
block—turn upfield
RH— Block 2nd man on or outside of 3—use
appropriate shoulder (start at 4-3 gap)
FB— Block 1st man outside of 2's block (any
way)

Play #90—"131 Pass"

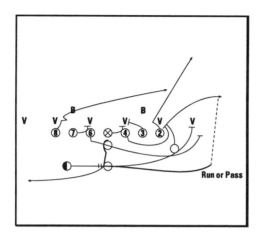

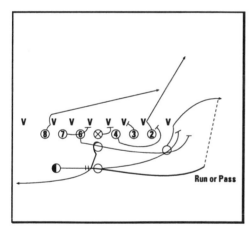

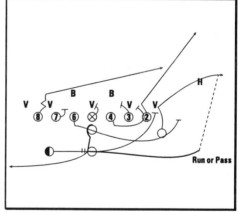

Blocking Rules:
2— Fake gap block—run flag pattern
3— Gap—inside
4— Pull—block 1st man outside of 3
5— On—right
6— Pull—react to LH's call—block on line of scrimmage or turn up
7— Block 1st man outside of 5
8— Run crossing pattern

Backfield Coaching Points:
QB— Reverse pivot—hand off to LH—fake bootleg at nine
LH— Carrier: Receive ball—if RH is open dump pass the ball—if defense drops off call "go"
RH— Fake gap block—run into flat at 5 yds
FB— Block 1st man outside of 3's block

Play #91—"Right 231 Pass"

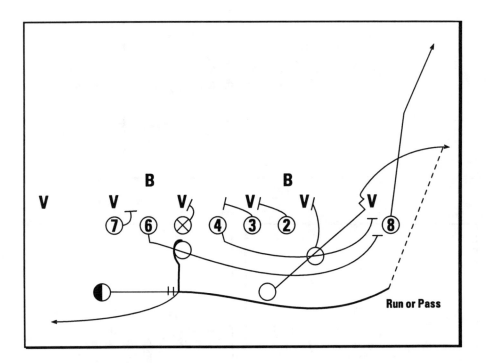

Blocking Rules:

2— Gap—on

3— Gap—inside

4— Pull—block 1st man outside of RH's block

5— Block man on—block right

6— Pull—one yard depth—personal escort (if LH calls go turn up field)

7— Block 1st man outside of 5

8— Opposite side—run flag pattern

Backfield Coaching Points:

QB— (RFB) Reverse pivot—hand off to LH— fake bootleg at nine

LH— Carrier: Receive ball—if FB is open dump ball—if defense drops off call "go"

RH— Block 1st man on or outside of 2

FB— Fake block on 1st man outside of RH's block—slip into flat at 5 yds

Play #92—"132 Keep Pass"

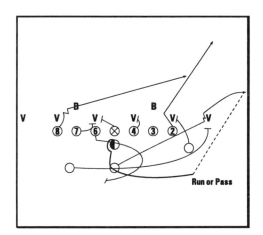

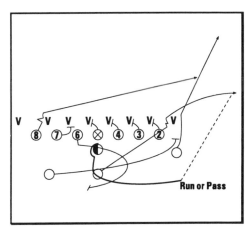

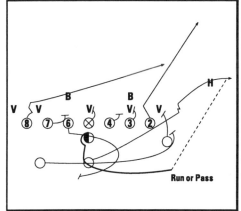

Blocking Rules:

2— Gap (If you block call "2")—no one in gap run flag pattern

3— Gap—area—on

4— Gap—area

5— Gap—area—left

6— Pull to outside leg of 3—2 steps depth—block back

7— Block 2nd man outside 5

8— Crossing pattern—split FB and deep receiver

Backfield Coaching Points:

QB— Reverse pivot—fake ball to LH and roll at one. Turn on speed no deeper than $5\frac{1}{2}$ yds—if they give it to you, run (use situation rule)

LH— Fake 132—flatten out behind 3 and block 1st man outside of RH's block (or 2's block)

RH— If end calls "2" run flag pattern—if you hear nothing block 1st man on or outside of end

FB— Run directly at 1st man outside of the RH—fake block—slip him and run into the flat at 5 yds.

Play #93—"Tight 132 Counter"

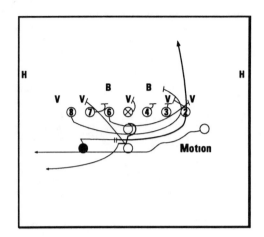

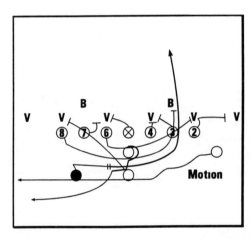

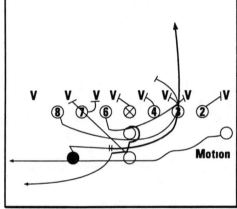

Blocking Rules:

2— Lead—block right
3— Gap—post—lead
4— Area—post
5— On—area—left
6— Inside out
7— Block 2nd man on or outside 5
8— Pull—block through hole and look inside

Backfield Coaching Points:

QB— Reverse pivot—hand off ball inside to
     LH—fake at nine
LH— Carrier: Step up and out with left foot—
     trail end as you receive inside hand off
RH— Fake at nine—leave in motion or fake
     one block and release
FB— Block check—dive for 6-7 seam—block
     1st man in area

Play #94—"Split 133"

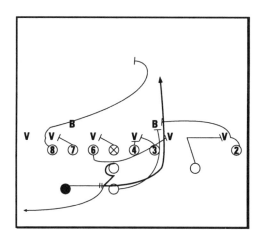

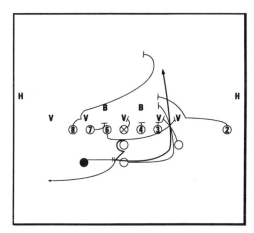

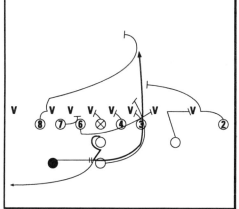

Blocking Rules:

2— Fake sweep block—wall off
3— Gap—post—lead
4— Gap—area—post
5— On—left
6— Pull—inside out
7— Block 2nd man on or outside of 5
8— Cut off

Backfield Coaching Points:

QB— Reverse pivot—hand ball off to left half—fake bootleg at nine

LH— Carrier: Receive hand off from QB—run parallel to L.O.S.—turn off post blocker

RH— Block lead—influence and block 1st man outside

FB— Run parallel to line—block through the hole and in

Play #95—"Right 296 Counter"

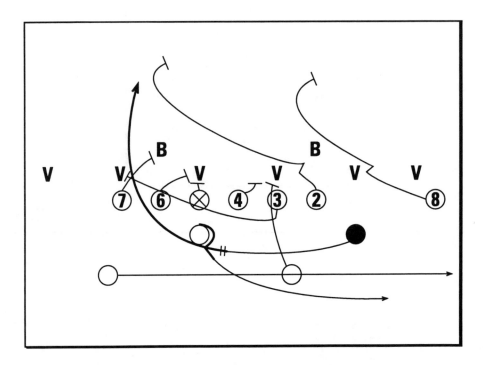

Blocking Rules:
2— Cut off
3— Pull—block inside out
4— Block post 4-5 gap—no man on or over 5 post—man on or over block man alone—area
5— Gap—post on or over—lead
6— Lead—block 1st man to left
7— Block across to backer
8— Opposite side—fake block down—cut off

Backfield Coaching Points:
QB— Sprints for RH's original position (fakes flare pass)—hands off inside to RH—fake fan keep at one
LH— Fake at one
RH— Carrier: Leave on the count—receive inside hand off
FB— Check—drive for tail of #3—block 1st man in area

Play #96—"Tight 137 Dive to the Left Half"

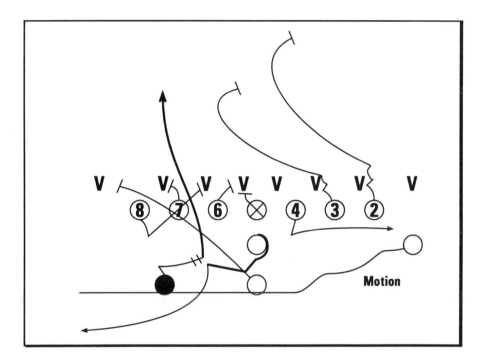

Blocking Rules:
2— Cut off
3— Cut off
4— Pull—fake away one play
5— On—over—left gap
6— Widen—block gap—pull away
7— Outside—on—over
8— Pull—block 1st man inside of 7

Backfield Coaching Points:
QB— Reverse pivot—hand ball off to RH—
    fake keep at nine
LH— Carrier: Step up and out with left foot—
    receive ball—use 8's block
RH— Leave in motion—fake at nine
FB— Cheat up 2 feet—drive for tail of 7—1st
    man outside of 7's block

Play #97—"Tight 138 Counter Criss Cross Bootleg Pass"

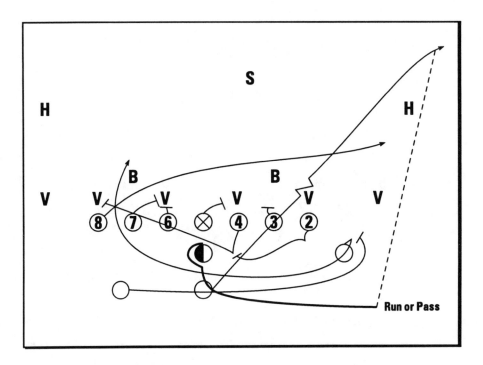

Blocking Rules:

2— Pull—fill hole left by the 4 man

3— Block 2nd man on or outside 5—head on right side

4— Block inside out as 38—keep head on outside

5— On—area—left

6— Gap—area—post

7— Gap—man on—you will not post but take him alone

8— Run across pattern—flat and fast

Backfield Coaching Points:

QB— Reverse pivot (as 132)—fake to LH as on 123 keep pass—place ball on hip and drift to about 8 yds—throw to open man

LH— Fake 138Ct criss cross—block 1st man outside of 3's block

RH— Fake 138Ct criss cross

FB— Drive for inside leg of #2—run under control for five yards—sprint for the flag looking over your right shoulder

Play #98—"Tight 134 Counter Jump Pass"

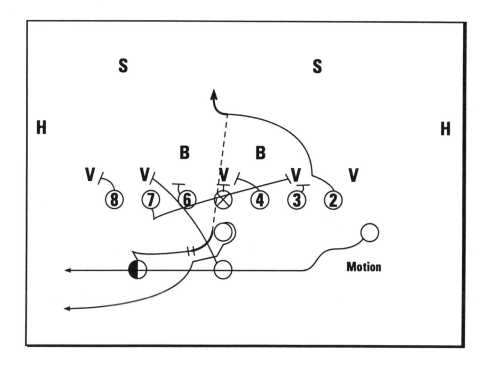

Blocking Rules:

2— Fake lead—run circular path to spot—receive pass

3— Block man on—man to your outside

4— Lead—block right

5— Gap—post (on or over)—lead

6— Block post man in 5-6 Gap—no man on or over post man on you—man on or over 5 block man on you or first man to your outside

7— Inside out

8— Block 2nd man outside of 6

Backfield Coaching Points:

QB— Reverse pivot (bring ball to LH)—hand off inside—fake bootleg at nine

LH— Rock weight on left foot (hesitate for ball)—receive ball—move to line jump and pass to RE

RH— Leave on motion—fake 34Ct

FB— Drive for 6-7 Seam—block 1st man in area

Play #99—"Tight 936 Counter Pass (RH Block—LH Flare)"

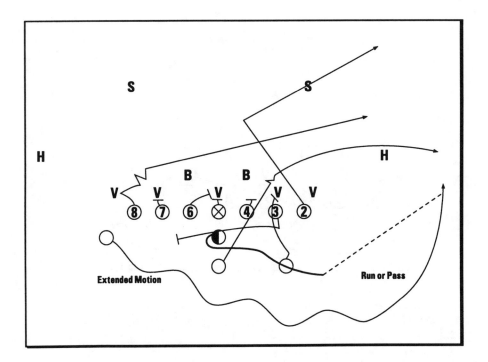

Blocking Rules:

2— Run normal bootleg pattern

3— Pull—block inside out

4— Same as 93Ct—block post (4-5 gap)—no man on or over 5 post—man on or over block man on block right

5— Same as 936Ct—block gap—post on or over—lead

6— Lead—area

7— On—area

8— Run end across pattern delayed

Backfield Coaching Points:

QB— Reverse pivot—move quickly to RH—fake 33 Dive—keep ball and throw to open man.

LH— Leave on early motion—get way out in front of QB—turn up into flat

RH— Fake 933 Dive—block 1st man outside of 3's block

FB— Dive for tail of 3 (follow RH)—take open spot and slip into flat at 5 yds.

Play #100—"Tight 134 Counter Jump Pass"

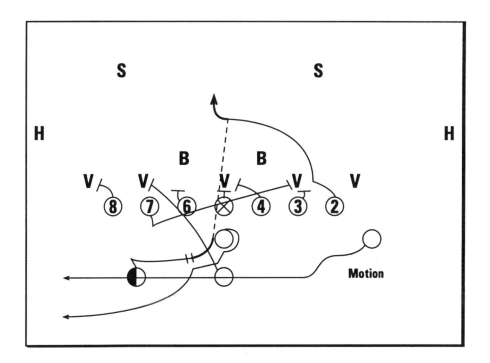

Blocking Rules:

2— Fake lead—run circular path to spot—receive pass
3— Block man on—man to your outside
4— Lead—block right
5— Gap—post (on or over)—lead
6— Block post man in 5-6 gap—no man on or over post man on you—man on or over 5 block man on you or first man to your outside
7— Inside out
8— Block 2nd man outside of 6

Backfield Coaching Points:

QB— Reverse pivot (bring ball to LH)—hand off inside—fake bootleg at nine
LH— Rock weight on left foot (hesitate for ball) receive ball—move to line jump and pass to RE
RH— Leave in motion—fake 34Ct
FB— Drive for 6-7 seam—block 1st man in area

Play #101—"Split 932 Counter Shuffle Pass"

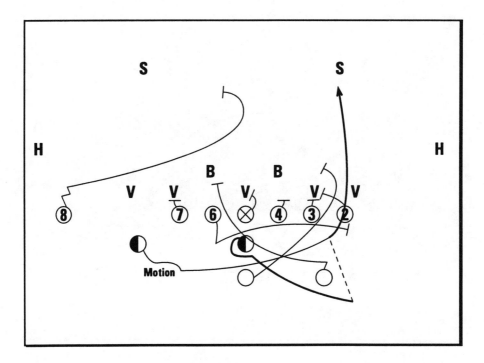

Blocking Rules:
2— Lead—block right
3— Gap—post—lead
4— Gap—area—post
5— On—area—check left
6— Inside out
7— Block 1st man outside of 6
8— (Split) Cut off

Backfield Coaching Points:
QB— Reverse pivot—fake 36Ct bootleg—get 7 yds depth—pass ball to LH
LH— Leave in one count motion—go in front of FB's original position—head for tail of 3—receive pass—turn up field
RH— Fake 36Ct
FB— Cheat to right and up—sprint for tail of 3—turn in—wall off

Harold R. "Tubby" Raymond is the head football coach at the University of Delaware—a position he has held since 1966. In that period, Raymond has led the Blue Hens to extraordinary accomplishments, including three national championships (1971, 1972 and 1979), 12 Lambert Cup Trophies, 13 NCAA playoff appearances, five Yankee Conference titles, and over 250 wins.

A 1950 graduate of the University of Michigan where he played both football and baseball for the Wolverines, Raymond has been honored numerous times for his coaching efforts, including being named NCAA Division II Coach of the year four times. A past president of the American Football Coaches Association, Raymond is widely renowned as one of the most outstanding football strategists in the history of the game.

Raymond has three children and eight grandchildren. Currently, he resides in Landerberg, Pennsylvania with his wife, Diane, and their daughter, Michelle.

Ted Kempski is the offensive coordinator for the University of Delaware football team. The starting quarterback on the 1961 and 1962 Blue Hen football teams, Kempski retuned to his alma mater in 1968 to coach the offensive backfield. In his 29 seasons on Tubby Raymond's staff, Kempski is credited with playing a key role in helping Delaware maintain its status as one of the premier rushing and total offense powerhouses in the nation.

Regarded as an exceptional teacher of football fundamentals, Kempski has helped three Blue Hen running backs become All-Americans—fullbacks Chuck Hall and Daryl Brown, and halfback Gardy Kahoe. A native of Wilmington, Delaware, where he was a multi-sport star in high school, Kempski currently resides in Elkton, Maryland with his wife Cathy. They have a son, Dan, and four grandchildren, Courtney, Katie, John and Zachary.

ADDITIONAL FOOTBALL RESOURCES FROM

- ### *THE DELAWARE WING-T: THE RUNNING GAME*
  by Harold "R" Tubby Raymond and Ted Kempski
  1998 ▪Paper▪ 164 pp
  ISBN 1-57167-166-8 ▪ $16.95

- ### *THE DELAWARE WING-T: THE PASSING GAME*
  by Harold "R" Tubby Raymond and Ted Kempski
  1998 ▪Paper▪ 152 pp
  ISBN 1-57167-165-x ▪ $16.95

- ### *THE DELAWARE WING-T: THE OPTION GAME*
  by Harold "R" Tubby Raymond and Ted Kempski
  1998 ▪Paper▪ 156 pp
  ISBN 1-57167-164-1 ▪ $16.95

- ### *101 DELAWARE WING-T DRILLS*
  by Harold "R" Tubby Raymond and Ted Kempski
  1998 ▪Paper▪ 116 pp
  ISBN 1-57167-162-5 - $16.95

TO PLACE YOUR ORDER:
U.S. customers call
TOLL FREE (800)327-5557,
or write
COACHES CHOICE Books, P.O. Box 647, Champaign, IL 61824-0647,
or FAX: (217) 359-5975